Critical Guides to Spanish Texts

69 García Lorca: Yerma

Critical Guides to Spanish Texts

EDITED BY ALAN DEYERMOND & STEPHEN HART

GARCÍA LORCA

Yerma

Andrew A. Anderson

Professor of Spanish
University of Virginia

Grant & Cutler Ltd
2003

© Grant & Cutler Ltd 2003

ISBN 0 7293 0431 0

DEPÓSITO LEGAL: V. 296 - 2003

Printed in Spain by
Artes Gráficas Soler, S.L., Valencia
for
GRANT & CUTLER LTD
55–57 GREAT MARLBOROUGH STREET, LONDON W1F 7AY

Contents

Prefatory Note

All quotations from the text of the play have been taken from the edition of *Yerma* prepared by Mario Hernández (Madrid: Alianza, 1998). This new, revised, and augmented edition by Hernández in Alianza's series 'El libro de bolsillo' / 'Biblioteca de autor' supersedes his previous edition of *Yerma* also published by Alianza ('Obras de Federico García Lorca', 1st ed. 1981, 2nd ed. 1984). As it incorporates the most up-to-date research on the manuscripts and early copies of the play, this edition offers the most reliable text. It also reproduces all the interviews given by Lorca which contain references to *Yerma*.

Page-number references both to the text of the play and to the interviews in the appendix to the edition are given parenthetically. (Readers should note that the pagination of the 1998 Alianza edition is different from previous Alianza editions, because of the incorporation of new material.) The figures in parentheses in italic type refer to the numbered works listed in the Bibliographical Note, and are followed where appropriate by a page number or numbers. On three occasions I have repeated a quotation from the text, because the same pieces of text are doing very different duty, and it is better for the reader to have the relevant passage immediately to hand, even at the expense of repetition.

I should like to express my thanks to Eric Southworth, who graciously fielded a number of questions I had in the course of the composition of this book and who was generous enough to read a draft version of it and make a number of valuable suggestions. My thanks are due also to Stephen Hart for his careful reading of the manuscript and his editorial support at all stages of this project.

1. Introduction

As was his wont, Lorca likely mapped out much of *Yerma* in his mind before putting pen to paper. This process of gestation seems to have begun some time in 1931, while he actually began work on the composition — that is, the writing-down — of the play early in the summer of 1933. He had Acts I and II finished by the time of his departure for Argentina at the end of September of that same year. Despite his stated intent to work on Act III during his six-month stay in Buenos Aires and Montevideo, this proved impossible, and so the play was not completed until after his return in the spring of 1934. By early August of that year he was giving private readings of the full draft of *Yerma*, though he doubtless tinkered with the text during the subsequent months, particularly during the period of rehearsals in late 1934.

The play immediately before *Yerma*, *Bodas de sangre*, had received its premiere in Madrid in March 1933, giving Lorca his first major success in the theatre. *Bodas de sangre* was restaged in Buenos Aires later that year, with a run of performances before his stay and another run during it, and this production proved to be extraordinarily popular. It is not hard to understand, therefore, why his next play was eagerly awaited. Indeed, it appears that the Argentinian actress Lola Membrives, whose company was performing *Bodas de sangre*, pressured Lorca to finish *Yerma* during those months in South America, but he did not do so, either because of the many other demands on his time, or because he preferred to see its debut in Spain with a different actress in the title role.

Yerma was premiered in Madrid at the Teatro Español on 29 December 1934 by Margarita Xirgu and her company. The play was enormously successful and enjoyed a long run, but at the same time stirred up considerable controversy. In the charged political climate of the times, the leading actress and the artistic director of the company, Cipriano Rivas Cherif, were perceived as having liberal, left-leaning, political affiliations. As a result, the conservative press tore into *Yerma* for its supposedly scabrous subject matter, but if anything this served only to heighten public interest in the play (*29; 33*). *Yerma* received one other staging during Lorca's lifetime. Performances were planned for Granada, Lorca's home town, during the Corpus Christi week of June 1935, but these were banned by the local authorities — understandably, given the essentially religious nature of the festivities and the controversial content of the play (*29*, p. 309). *Yerma* was put on again, once more by Margarita Xirgu and her company, at the Teatro Barcelona in Barcelona, debuting on 17 September 1935. As was only to be expected, it proved to be extremely popular also with Catalan audiences. Later that autumn, Xirgu took the same production to Valencia and other cities in the region.

Yerma is a play from what we consider today the mature period of Lorca's theatrical output — the middle 1930s, though this perspective is undoubtedly skewed by his untimely death in 1936 at the age of 38. As already noted, *Yerma* was preceded by *Bodas de sangre* (1933), and it was followed first by *Doña Rosita la soltera* (1935) and then by *La casa de Bernarda Alba* (1936, first performance 1945). Had the Civil War not broken out in the summer of 1936, Lorca would have seen four major plays premiered in as many years.

Lorca identified *Yerma* as the middle play of a trilogy of tragedies that he planned to write, often identified by subsequent critics as the 'rural tragedies' and sometimes as the 'folk tragedies'. In ancient Greece it was the usual practice for playwrights to stage sets of three tragedies — known as the trilogy — and so Lorca's adoption of this model is one more indication of the connections that he sought to create between his own works and classical tragedy (chapter 9). In interviews he gave periodic reports on the progress of his trilogy:

> Ahora voy a terminar *Yerma*, una segunda tragedia mía.
> La primera fue *Bodas de sangre*. (150)

Mientras tanto, yo quiero dar al teatro tragedias. *Yerma*, que está acabándose, será la segunda. (151)

Mi trayectoria en el teatro […], yo la veo perfectamente clara. Quisiera terminar la trilogía de *Bodas de sangre*, *Yerma* y *El drama de las hijas de Loth*. Me falta esta última. (157)

Yerma marca el punto central en la trilogía iniciada hace dos años con *Bodas de sangre*, y que terminaré en *Las hijas de Lot*. (161)

Ahora, a terminar la trilogía que empezó con *Bodas de sangre*, sigue con *Yerma* y acabará con *La destrucción de Sodoma*… (164)

A *Yerma* seguirá el estreno de *Doña Rosita o El lenguaje de las flores*, en tanto continúa con formidable empeño creador su obra titulada *Las hijas de Lot*, que sin aparecer en una relación directa con *Bodas de sangre* y *Yerma*, vendrá a completar con ellas un ciclo dramático de apasionadas protagonistas.[1]

Two things are quite clear: the trilogy was to be made up of *Bodas de sangre*, *Yerma* and a third play, and in all Lorca's public pronouncements that third play was identified as *Las hijas de Lot* / *La destrucción de Sodoma* (obviously the same work). There is no recorded, first-hand evidence that he, at some point, decided to substitute *La casa de Bernarda Alba* for *Las hijas de Lot* and make it the third and final tragedy in the trilogy, but nonetheless this certainly seems to be the case. There are good reasons to believe that such a change occurred, not least the fact that *La casa de Bernarda Alba* inhabits a world — a small town or village, situated in a rural, farming community — barely dissimilar to those of *Bodas de sangre*

---

[1]Sánchez-Trincado, 'Hablando con García Lorca', *Hoja Literaria* (Barcelona), 1.1 (1 de octubre de 1935), p. 1; an interview not collected by Hernández. The journalist has reported Lorca's words to him indirectly; the original text reads 'sus obras tituladas', clearly a typographical error.

and *Yerma*, whereas the overtly biblical subject matter of *Las hijas de Lot* seems to jar when set beside those first two plays in the sequence.[2] As things stand, therefore, the play under consideration in this Guide may safely be approached as the middle tragedy in a trilogy composed of *Bodas de sangre*, *Yerma*, and *La casa de Bernarda Alba* (*27*, pp. 157, 174).

---

[2]It seems that Lorca eventually settled on the title *La destrucción de Sodoma*, that he had the plot worked out in his mind, and that he may even have written part of the play; however, only half a page of manuscript has survived. Furthermore, *La destrucción de Sodoma* would appear to take its place within a new biblical trilogy that he was planning shortly before he was killed, to be composed of that play, *Caín y Abel* and *Thamar y Amnón*.

2. The Setting, Characters, Relationships

The action of the play is set in a village somewhere in Spain. There are no indications as to the date (though there are several mentions of the amount of time that elapses during the course of the play), nor are there any precise pointers to the location of the village (*48*, p. 19). It is quite easy to imagine that the action could be more or less contemporary with the composition of the play, but given the unchanging nature of living and working conditions in rural Spanish society until recent times, it could just as well be set back in some prior century; in other words, the action is essentially timeless. Likewise, given Lorca's background, he probably drew on his first-hand experience of life in the Andalusian countryside, but there is little in the text that specifically situates the action in the south of Spain, save, perhaps, the presence of olive trees.

Indeed, we learn very little about the topography, layout, or size of this nameless village where Yerma lives. It is small enough for everybody to know everybody else's business (chapter 3), it has some hills (55, 96), and, crucially for this essentially agricultural community, it is blessed with a river. There are mentions of a 'río', 'arroyo' and even a 'torrente' (47, 63, 92, 96), which all probably describe the same watercourse that is to be found down in a valley and at a little distance from the centre of town (96). There are mills, probably watermills rather than windmills, given their proximity to the river (47), there are irrigation channels ('acequias', 50, 100) fed by the river, and there is a spring or fountain (76).

Land in Spain is split into two basic categories, *tierra de secano* and *tierra de riego*, that is, areas that have to rely exclusively on rainfall for water and areas that can be irrigated. Given the climate of this Mediterranean country, it is easy to appreciate how water becomes the most important and precious commodity for farmers and *tierra de riego* is much more productive in terms of crop

yield (and hence, logically, much more valuable as an asset). As
river levels dropped in the summer months farmers in a given area
would be allocated a strict schedule governing when they could open
the sluice gates of the irrigation channels, and it is in this light that
we can understand the following exchange between Yerma and Juan:

> YERMA: ¿Te espero?

> JUAN: No. Estaré toda la noche regando. Viene poca
> agua, es mía hasta la salida del sol y tengo que
> defenderla de los ladrones. (62)

While concrete details about the village are extremely scarce,
the play is a little more forthcoming about the range of agricultural
activities. Thus 'las cosas de la labor' (33) can be understood more
specifically as ploughing with teams of oxen (32, 91), growing wheat
(70), tending the olive groves (46, 53), pruning apple trees (76–77),
and herding flocks of sheep (69, 91–94; *41*, p. 58).

Within this setting we encounter the primary characters.
Yerma's unusual name has been made up by Lorca — it is not found
in the repertory of Spanish first names. Rather it is derived from the
adjective *yermo*, *-a*, meaning barren or desert-like, and normally
applied to land; as such, it marks her from the outset as an archetypal
being. However, in other respects, Yerma possesses a conventional,
naturalistic background. She is the daughter of Enrique the shepherd
and an unnamed mother (34, 47), among her siblings she can count
at least one sister (probably elder) and one brother (42, 80), both of
whom have children of their own, and she has at least one uncle (48).
More pointedly, the Vieja of Act I, Scene ii notes that her father was
'buena gente' (47) and that her extended family is numerous (117);
Yerma herself refers to 'mi padre, que me dejó su sangre de padre de
cien hijos' (104). At the opening of the play she is still young (52)
and is addressed by the Vieja as 'muchacha' (46, 49, 50), putting her
likely in her late teens or early twenties — her near contemporary the
Muchacha 2ª is nineteen (55). Furthermore, both the Vieja and
Víctor describe her as physically attractive ('hermosa' 46, 49, 51,
57).

Yerma is in many ways defined by her overwhelming desire to have children; this feature is so central to her character that it will be treated at length in a discussion of the themes of the play (chapter 6). With regard to her other traits, we know that she is an obedient daughter who readily accepts the husband her father selects for her (50). In Act I she is strongly associated with the activity of sewing (31, 36, 43, 45), a traditionally feminine skill; lacking children, she has had plenty of free time to hone her ability. Furthermore, she is characterized as a 'flor abierta' and 'inocente' (51), suggesting guilelessness and an innocence bordering on naiveté. Yerma describes herself as 'vergonzosa' (50), which we can translate as shy, bashful, retiring, while at the same time the term implies a degree of sexual modesty or reserve (chapter 3); indeed, later she asserts that 'no soy una casada indecente' and that 'siempre he tenido asco de las mujeres calientes' (98; *38*, p. 75; *39*, p. 25). This puritanical viewpoint may well be related to her upbringing, to judge by the Vieja's description of Yerma's father's austere lifestyle, which is the diametric opposite of her own (47–48); indeed, the Vieja preferred not to marry an uncle of Yerma's, who apparently shared his brother's dour outlook (48). Overall, Yerma has a very strong sense of family, reflected in her use of the word 'casta', a noun meaning breeding, lineage, family line, ancestry, but also a word which as an adjective in its feminine form means chaste (*19*, p. 200). Thus 'casta' in both its literal meaning and its punning secondary meaning is intimately connected with an equally strong sense of honour, understood primarily as integrity — a personal code of moral conduct (see chapters 3 and 6; *14*, p. 89). More than once Yerma chafes at the constrictions imposed by honour in its social dimension as reputation, and while she sometimes draws unwelcome attention to herself by eccentric behaviour (as defined by the norms of the society in which she lives), throughout the play she continues to affirm the inherent integrity (and chastity) of all her actions (61, 86, 99, 103, 118). Finally, we see that she is a woman of considerable resolve and courage, when occasion demands (49, 95).

Juan is a dedicated and successful farmer. We find out very little about his family, save that he has two unmarried and devout sisters, the Cuñadas (see below). The Vieja's opinion of him and his family is decidedly biased: first she insinuates that Juan is sterile by including him, in so many words, among 'los hombres de simiente podrida' (52); later she tells Yerma that 'ni su padre, ni su abuelo, ni su bisabuelo se portaron como hombres de casta' (117). But we need to remember that in this second instance the Vieja is trying to procure Yerma as a mate for her own son, and that she overlooks or deliberately ignores the fact that Juan's father managed to have a minimum of three children. Juan possesses a good deal of land, including wheat fields, pasture meadows, olive groves, and apple orchards (46, 76, 77, 84, 103); he also has oxen for ploughing (85) and owns sheep and buys more from Víctor (45, 91–92, 98). Through the course of the action of the play, his crops and livestock thrive (33), he expands his holdings, and by the end he is considered well-off (92; *41*, p. 60). At the same time, he is also depicted as being overly interested in monetary profit and gloating over the results (45, 98). But his material success is not easily won; he is an extremely, perhaps excessively, hard worker who spends long hours in the fields, sometimes staying there overnight (32, 33, 44–45, 62, 65, 76, 77). This demanding work is seen to have an impact on his physique: for Yerma he is gaunt and pale, but Juan interprets this differently, depicting himself as lean but wiry (32). He appears to be a stolid, straight-faced individual, rarely joking or laughing, and this is described as a 'dryness' or 'sadness' (58). On the other hand, the majority of the villagers consider him a decent man and a good provider, and Víctor comments on his probity in financial dealings (91, 98).

Unlike Yerma, Juan is not at all bothered by their lack of children; indeed, he views them as costly and troublesome, and at the very end of the play he asserts that he is actually happier without them (33, 79, 99, 121–22). It must be said that for a farmer with considerable holdings of land and livestock, this attitude is not what one would expect (*1*, p. 32; *2*, p. 30; *37*, p. 286). Conventionally, a farmer in Juan's position would want sons who would help him in the fields and to whom he could hand on the results of his labours — compare the attitudes of both Madre and Padre in *Bodas de sangre*.

Víctor makes this precise point when he advises Yerma: 'Dile a tu marido que piense menos en el trabajo. Quiere juntar dinero y lo juntará, pero ¿a quién lo va a dejar cuando se muera?' (45). It is conceivable that his overt attitude is only a smokescreen hiding deep and dark concerns about the lack of offspring and his own apparent inability to father them, but this really does not seem to be the case. Juan is repeatedly depicted as content with the way things are; rather than worrying about questions of inheritance he believes that given all his hard work he is deserving of a quiet life and some personal satisfaction (35, 76). Such a stance is consistent with other related traits, such as a recognition of some of his flaws (79), pragmatically modest expectations (121), and a certain fatalistic resignation — 'Cada año seré más viejo' (33). Overall, then, he comes across as a rather pale personality, both literally and figuratively.[3] However, in his views about the place of women and honour Juan is strongly opinionated and utterly conventional. His pithy phrase 'las ovejas en el redil y las mujeres en su casa' (78) sums up his philosophy on the first matter; likewise, he considers himself as coming from an honourable family (77, 103) and is concerned about his reputation in the village (101).

At the start of the play Yerma and Juan have been husband and wife for more or less exactly two years (33), and as we have seen, it was an arranged marriage. Yerma's father's reasoning in selecting Juan is likely to have been purely economic: marrying off a shepherd's daughter to a hard-working farmer with considerable holdings of arable land would have been perceived as a highly

---

[3]Lorca was asked by a newspaper reporter why he had not made Juan more manly and assertive, and his reply is worth quoting: '—*[...] he echado de menos un hombre con más seguridad en la réplica y con más conciencia de su destino que el marido.* | —Si pongo un hombre de pelo en pecho, me ahoga el drama de *Yerma*. El marido es "un hombre débil y sin voluntad". No lo he querido presentar de otra manera porque hubiera sido desplazar el drama de la protagonista, con lo que habría resultado una obra distinta de la que concebí. Lo que me propuse hacer fue el drama de la casada seca solamente' (196–97).

advantageous match. Yerma herself would have had little say in the matter, and while she stresses that she entered into the marriage willingly and indeed joyously (34), her primary, if not exclusive, motivation from the outset was the opportunity to bear children (50). We do not really know how she felt about Juan as a person, and it is quite likely that they had not spent much time together beforehand; further, given her shy, retiring, bashful character it seems certain that she would have had few or no significant romantic experiences in the years preceding her marriage. As for Juan, he acknowledges that what he sought all along was 'la casa, la tranquilidad y una mujer. Pero nada más. [...] Como todos' (121–22). Broadly speaking, then, each views the other as a means to certain ends, but those ends coincide only very partially: for Yerma, Juan will be a provider, supplying her with a place to live, clothes, food, etc. (86), as well as conferring the status and respectability of marriage, but above all he will serve to give her children (50; *17*, pp. 716, 720; *26*, p. 137). Juan's goals are to have someone to run the household, to cook, wash and clean, to provide companionship, and to satisfy his sexual needs (*37*, p. 287; *41*, p. 64). Hence, as Sullivan points out, neither the motives of Yerma nor of Juan are other-oriented (*49*, p. 275).

Not surprisingly, the dynamic of their relationship changes considerably over the more than five years of their marriage. In Act I, two years in, there is already some friction between them. For instance, in Juan's opinion Yerma is overly solicitous (33), but clearly the main source of irritation is Yerma's insistent return to the topic of her future motherhood, as exemplified in the following exchange:

YERMA: Nadie se casó con más alegría. Y sin embargo...

JUAN: Calla.

YERMA: Y sin embargo...

JUAN: Calla. Demasiado trabajo tengo yo con oír en todo momento... (34–35)

Indeed, Yerma later admits that 'con mi marido no hablo de otra cosa' (49). Juan does recognize that Yerma loves him (34), but it appears that this is more an act of will on her part than anything spontaneous or deeply felt (35). For as Yerma confesses to the Vieja, she does not experience any physical sensations of sexual excitement when she is with her husband (49); she had an inkling of that kind of feeling only with Víctor when she was a teenager and 'mi marido es otra cosa' (50). During these first years of marriage, then, Yerma has fulfilled her wifely duties around the house and has complied with Juan's preference that she should stay at home and venture out into the street as little as possible (35). But there are signs that this is beginning to change at the very end of Act I, when he comes across her chatting with Víctor at the roadside (61–62). Juan reprimands Yerma and expresses his concerns about gossip (see chapter 3); she then steers the conversation around to her childlessness but he refuses to be drawn into yet another discussion. She backs down and offers a conciliatory gesture ('Está bien. ¿Te espero?' [62]), but the scene ends with Juan informing Yerma that he will be out all night (to irrigate his fields), and hence she will sleep alone — a pointedly significant arrangement in the context of the preceding exchange. One wonders to what extent Yerma's mono-thematic harping on is actually bringing about exactly the opposite result, driving Juan away rather than bringing him to their shared bed (*26*, p. 145; *37*, p. 291); likewise, one is led to speculate to what extent Juan's endless duties in the fields are a pretext to stay away, an excuse to take a break from Yerma's equally endless nagging (*41*, p. 61).

In Act II the situation has deteriorated and the breakdown of trust has led Juan to bring in his two spinster sisters to live with them, evidently to act as watchdogs over Yerma's behaviour so that he can carry on his agricultural labours without having to worry about what is going on at home and where Yerma is (64–65). But the Cuñadas prove to be less than competent, and at the opening of Act II, Scene ii Yerma has again gone missing, though only, as it turns out, to fetch water from the fountain (76–77). Exactly the same exchange as at the end of Act I plays itself out again, with Yerma asking if Juan will stay at home and his reply that he will be out all night — this time watching over the livestock (77). The crucial difference is that Yerma's comments are now barbed with acrimony and sarcasm:

> JUAN: Cada hombre tiene su vida.
>
> YERMA: Y cada mujer la suya. No te pido yo que te quedes. Aquí tengo todo lo que necesito. Tus hermanas me guardan bien. Pan tierno y requesón y cordero asado como yo aquí, y pasto lleno de rocío tus ganados en el monte. Creo que puedes vivir en paz. (77)

As the conversation develops, the misalignment between the two of them becomes ever more apparent. Yerma states that she would happily conform to Juan's view of the woman's place and role if only there were some life — i.e. children — in the house; as it is, she stoically but unhappily accepts her lot: 'En nada te ofendo. Vivo sumisa a ti y lo que sufro lo guardo pegado a mis carnes' (78). Juan, on the other hand, believes himself unjustly attacked, as he has been utterly open and consistent in his attitudes since day one: '¿Es que no conoces mi modo de ser? [...] ¿No me has oído decir esto siempre?' (78) — Yerma therefore knew what she was getting herself into. Further, he finds it impossible to understand why she keeps returning to this one topic, pointing out how well he treats her and cares for her generally (79), which is an aspect of their relationship that Yerma barely acknowledges (*41*, pp. 61–62). The argument develops into a series of complaints and accusations and counteraccusations (80–81), but ends — for the moment — with Juan apologizing and Yerma asking that they drop the subject (82). This has been interpreted as demonstrating Juan's weak will, but it could just as easily show that Juan still has feelings for Yerma, which might explain why it appears to someone outside the family like María that 'tu marido te sigue queriendo' (86).

By Act III a considerable gulf has opened between them. Yerma recognizes that she does not love Juan at all (99) and she complains that on the rare occasions that they dutifully have sexual intercourse, it is a cold and passionless activity (98). For his part,

Juan rebukes Yerma for what he sees as her sly and deceitful ways (102) as well as her erratic behaviour, which he finds suspicious as well as likely to attract public attention (103). But what is really intolerable for Juan are the nights, when he is trying to sleep, while Yerma lies awake 'mirándome con dos agujas, pasando las noches en vela con los ojos abiertos al lado mío, y llenando de malos suspiros mis almohadas', 'una mujer que te quiere meter los dedos dentro del corazón' (102). Of course, this conflict culminates in a terrible act of violence, the significance of which will be discussed fully in chapter 8.

The third important character in the play is Víctor, though his background and character are much less fleshed out than either Yerma or Juan. He is a childhood friend of Yerma, from the same village. He is a shepherd, as apparently are his whole family of father and brothers (88–89). At his first appearance the stage directions describe him thus: 'Es profundo y lleno de firme gravedad' (44), but he is also of a happy disposition with a good singing voice (57–58). He is well-liked in the village (90), and like Yerma he is obedient to his father (88–89). He is a conformist and something of a fatalist (90–91). Overall, then, he is a person of probity; his business deals with Juan go smoothly (45, 91), he is joyful when he (mistakenly) believes that Yerma is pregnant (44), and while he is friendly with her, he also observes every propriety during their conversations.

In some respects, then, Víctor and Juan are not that different: they are honest, hard-working and generally respected in the village, they try to fit in, they accept the social system and its *mores*, and they are resigned to their lot in life. However, a strong contrast is drawn in terms of Yerma's physical and emotional responses to each of them and in the particular way they earn their livelihood. While Víctor is a shepherd, Juan is primarily a farmer of fields and orchards, though he does also own livestock and indeed buys more head of sheep from Víctor (*50*, pp. 46–47). In these two modes of agriculture it is quite possible to detect echoes of that archetypal distinction between Abel and Cain: 'And Abel was a keeper of sheep, but Cain was a tiller of the ground' (Genesis 4.2) (*21*, p. 66; *31*, p. 13). Inasmuch as Cain kills Abel in the biblical story, we can perhaps say that Juan figuratively kills Víctor in two complementary ways: he displaces him as Yerma's bridegroom, even though Víctor was close to her when they were younger and he is a shepherd, like Yerma's own father, and Juan buys all Víctor's flocks just as he is leaving with his brothers, making them Yerma's as well as Juan's (91–92). Ironically, Víctor is certainly not the victor in this romantic and socio-economic contest.

Yerma's and Víctor's relationship dates back to childhood. When questioned by the Vieja, Yerma recalls two episodes, once when she and Víctor danced and she was unable to speak a word, and another time when he helped her jump over an irrigation channel and she started to tremble (50). There are, in addition, three moments in the course of the play when we see Yerma interacting with Víctor. We must be careful, though, not to read too much into these scenes, as it is far from clear how conscious Yerma is of her own thoughts and feelings, just as it is impossible to determine if they are specifically focussed on Víctor as an individual or if they correspond more generally to Víctor as a sympathetic and attractive man on to whom she projects certain fantasies (*12*, pp. 24–25).

Their first meeting is relatively brief, and as Víctor leaves, a stage direction indicates that 'YERMA, que en actitud pensativa se levanta y acude al sitio donde ha estado VÍCTOR y respira fuertemente como si respirara aire de montaña' (45). Their second encounter is a little more charged, with numerous awkward pauses and silences and Yerma thinking first that Víctor has a burn or scar on his cheek and then that she can hear the distant crying of an infant (58–60); midway through the conversation a stage direction notes that 'el silencio se acentúa y sin el menor gesto comienza una lucha entre los dos personajes' (59). Finally, Víctor comes to take his leave and again the stage directions indicate that under the surface Yerma is disturbed and saddened, perhaps regretting his departure but at the same time recognizing that nothing can be done to prevent it (88–93).

While these scenes contain a variety of clear intimations that Víctor would in all likelihood have made a much better match for Yerma than Juan does, we should probably not overinterpret this, as some critics do (cf. 7, p. 469). Víctor is, after all, by definition unavailable. Furthermore, it never becomes clear what Víctor's present-day attitude towards Yerma is, whether he is more than content simply to remain a friend of the family or whether his moral code prevents him from even hinting at stronger feelings for a married woman. For instance, is he really bound to carry out the wishes of his aging father in leaving the village for good (88–89), or does he seize on the opportunity as an excuse to put distance between them? Even at the moment of farewell, does he entertain some ill-defined hope that Yerma will offer an eleventh-hour profession of love?:

> (VÍCTOR *da la vuelta y, a un movimiento imperceptible de* YERMA, *se vuelve.*)
>
> VÍCTOR: ¿Decías algo?
>
> YERMA (*Dramática.*): Salud dije.
>
> VÍCTOR: Gracias. (93)

At all events, things never progress beyond a certain embarrassed awkwardness or stiffness and the suggestion of unspoken ideas and emotions. Indeed, it is impossible to imagine things as being any other way, given Yerma's redoubtable sense of family, honour and integrity, and Víctor's probity and conformism. Nonetheless, it appears that even these chance encounters and tentative conversations between the two of them have given rise to a certain amount of gossip in the village. Although names are not named, it is more than likely that Lavandera 4ª is alluding to Víctor:

> LAVANDERA 1ª: Pero ¿vosotras la habéis visto con otro?
>
> LAVANDERA 4ª: Nosotras no, pero las gentes sí.
>
> LAVANDERA 1ª: ¡Siempre las gentes!
>
> LAVANDERA 5ª: Dicen que en dos ocasiones.

LAVANDERA 2ª: ¿Y qué hacían?

LAVANDERA 4ª: Hablaban.

LAVANDERA 1ª: Hablar no es pecado.

LAVANDERA 4ª: Hay una cosa en el mundo que es la mirada. […] Ella lo mira.

LAVANDERA 1ª: ¿Pero a quién?

LAVANDERA 4ª: A uno. (66–67)

The remainder of the characters are decidedly secondary. The two Cuñadas, also described in the stage directions as Hermana Mayor and Hermana Menor, are Juan's sisters and hence Yerma's sisters-in-law. They are unmarried and before coming to live with Juan and Yerma had been in charge of looking after the church, presumably sweeping it, cleaning, making flower arrangements, and so on (64). Whitewashing, cleaning and polishing also seem to play a large part in their activity at Yerma's house (68). They dress in mourning black and are clearly intended by Lorca to appear as *beatas*, highly devout women, as is underlined by the comments of the Lavanderas (64–65; *25*, p. 141). Perhaps their most notable feature is that they are almost entirely silent; when addressed they usually answer with gestures (76, 77), they glide on and off stage like shadows, hovering about the house, and between them they utter just five words: '¡Yerma!' three times at the end of Act II (94), and 'Aquí está' (101) in Act III, Scene i.

Most of the remaining minor characters are either (a) other village-dwellers, or (b) people attending the *romería* in Act III, Scene ii. There are three young married friends or acquaintances of Yerma: María, who in Act I, Scene i has just discovered that she is pregnant, Muchacha 1ª, who has one child, and Muchacha 2ª, who has reluctantly married, is childless but has no desire to have children. The Vieja is a stranger to Yerma until their meeting in Act I, Scene ii, though they soon discover they know a number of people in common. The Vieja has lived a full life, with two husbands and fourteen children (six of whom died) (48).[4] She describes her lifestyle thus: 'yo he sido una mujer de faldas en el aire, he ido flechada a la tajada de melón, a la fiesta, a la torta de azúcar' (48). She reappears in Act III, Scene ii, where she suggests to Yerma that she come and live with her and one of her sons, who is looking for a wife (116–19). The six Lavanderas, 1ª, 2ª, 3ª, 4ª, 5ª and 6ª, are representative of the mass of the rest of the villagers. They function as a group but are differentiated by their attitudes towards Yerma and Juan: 1ª blames Juan, 4ª blames Yerma, and the others subscribe to differing degrees to these two extreme viewpoints. Dolores, the mother of Muchacha 2ª, is described in the stage directions as a 'conjuradora' (95), that is a 'wise woman' who knows prayers, spells, herbal remedies and magic potions. She is assisted by two neighbour women (87) who appear in Act III, Scene i as Vieja 1ª and Vieja 2ª; these are not to be confused with the Vieja of Act I and again of Act III, Scene ii, where Lorca describes her as 'la Vieja alegre del primer acto' (107, 116).[5] The *romería* scene, the last in the play, is much more densely populated than any of the others. Besides Yerma and Juan, María, Muchacha 1ª and the Vieja reappear from earlier scenes; new secondary characters include the mask-wearing Macho and Hembra, as well as six women, three of whom are identified as Mujer 1ª, 2ª and 3ª, two men, Hombre 1º and 2º, seven Muchachas, and several children — Niños — one of whom has a speaking part.[6]

---

[4]Lorca's arithmetic is faulty: on the previous page the Vieja says she has nine (surviving) sons and no daughters (47) (*5*, p. 217).

[5]In the dramatis personae she appears as Vieja Pagana (30).

[6]There are several inconsistencies between the dramatis personae and the actual character count; María's child in arms, the two Viejas who assist Dolores, and the seven Muchachas are all missing from the list of characters, the list specifies two women while a total of six appear, and it calls for three men while only two appear.

3. Rural Society and its Values

Rural society is generally known for its conservative, traditional values, and Yerma's village is no exception. Broadly speaking, then, in such a community as this there is strong resistance to change, there is little contact with or influence from the outside world, the land, hard work, marriage and family are the cornerstones of daily life, sex-role stereotypes are maintained and defended, and what is considered moral, conformist behaviour is the norm. Articulating and regulating this society there is a complex, interlocking system of institutions, *mores*, beliefs and priorities, and informing all of these there is an underlying tendency to perpetuate and defend the *status quo*.[7]

Marriage lies at the very hub of this system. Almost all women can expect to get married (*17*, p. 716); they typically marry young, often 'married off' by their parents in arranged alliances, which was the case with Yerma. As the Muchacha 2ª complains:

> ...me han casado. Se casan todas. Si seguimos así, no va a haber solteras más que las niñas. [...] Pero las viejas se empeñan en todas estas cosas. Yo tengo diecinueve años y no me gusta guisar, ni lavar. Bueno, pues todo el día he de estar haciendo lo que no me gusta. ¿Y para qué? ¿Qué necesidad tiene mi marido de ser mi marido? [...] Tonterías de los viejos. (54–55)

---

[7]For a classic anthropological study of Andalusian village life, which throws light on much of Lorca's work, see Julian A. Pitt-Rivers, *The People of the Sierra*, 2nd ed. (Chicago: University of Chicago Press, 1971). For an excellent study of village life and women's roles, see *17*.

After the wedding, the husband takes over from the father as the person in charge, and the daughter-now-wife remains in a distinctly subordinate role. Two of the bluntest statements exemplifying this feature of the social structure come from Juan: 'Las ovejas en el redil y las mujeres en su casa' (78); 'no debía decirte "perdóname", sino obligarte, encerrarte, porque para eso soy el marido' (82). A more extreme manner of conceiving this relationship envisages the wife as the husband's possession, his chattel, over whom he has complete dominion, and precisely this notion underpins Yerma's defiant and provocative complaint to Juan: 'haz conmigo lo que quieras, que soy tu mujer, pero guárdate de poner nombre de varón sobre mis pechos' (103). Interestingly, Juan's attitude is essentially seconded by Víctor, who appears to share a similar if less overtly authoritarian world view: 'La acequia por su sitio, el rebaño en el redil, la luna en el cielo y el hombre con su arado' (91). Compare, too, the lines from the Macho's song: 'Los maridos son toros, / el varón siempre manda' (115).

Men give the orders and they are also the breadwinners, while women are supposed to meekly obey, carry out their appointed tasks — which are largely of a domestic nature, and, above all, have children (*17*, pp. 716, 720; *41*, pp. 58, 60, 65). Childbearing is their primary goal within marriage, and it defines the woman's role: to reproduce, and then to take care of the household and the children within it. In an agricultural community this would be viewed not only as right and natural but also as desirable, for at a relatively young age boys would start assisting their fathers in the fields, and girls their mothers in the house. As the Vieja comments, she has a husband and numerous sons who all work, but she has no daughters to help her, so she is kept perpetually busy: 'aquí me tienes a mí de un lado para otro' (47).

Yerma is well aware of all these unwritten rules, and while she certainly perceives a clear imbalance in them, she is nevertheless generally accepting: 'Justo. Las mujeres dentro de sus casas' (78); 'Los hombres tienen otra vida: los ganados, los árboles, las conversaciones; y las mujeres no tenemos más que ésta de la cría y el cuido de la cría' (79). Later, though, her stance begins to change. On the one hand, the contrast between men and women's very nature seems to be more stark:

> VÍCTOR: Es todo lo mismo. Las mismas ovejas tienen
> la misma lana.

> YERMA: Para los hombres, sí, pero las mujeres somos
> otra cosa. Nunca oí decir a un hombre comiendo: '¡Qué
> buenas son estas manzanas!' Vais a lo vuestro sin
> reparar en las delicadezas. (89)

On the other, it appears to Yerma that she is herself becoming more manly:

> Muchas noches bajo yo a echar la comida a los bueyes,
> que antes no lo hacía porque ninguna mujer lo hace, y
> cuando paso por lo oscuro del cobertizo mis pasos me
> suenan a pasos de hombre. (85)

In social terms, then, Yerma is seen — and sees herself — first and foremost as a wife, and she is a member of a society that holds firm to a series of ideas about the institution of marriage, its nature and purposes, and the respective duties and obligations of the two spouses. The great majority of those ideas are, in turn, rooted in traditional Catholic doctrine, whence they have permeated the social system (*19*, p. 199; *26*, p. 140 n65; *34*, p. 227). Catholic teaching on the subject of matrimony therefore plays a critical if mainly hidden or unspoken role, for it establishes a set of goals and modes of conduct to which Yerma largely subscribes, even if her personal interpretation of some of these appears to be partial, exaggerated or extreme (see chapter 6).

Various texts can offer us a window into the intricacies of this view of marriage. Morris quotes the catechism, from a text dating from 1941, which prescribes:

> El cristiano debe respetar la pureza de su cuerpo, que es
> templo del Espíritu Santo. Así, que cualquiera acción fea
> consigo o con otra persona, es pecado mortal.
>
> También es pecado entretenerse en malos pensamientos
> o deseos de cosas torpes. (*38*, pp. 75, 81 n19)

Martínez Lacalle looks to the 'version of canon law then in force
(*Código de Derecho Canónico*, canon 1013, paragraph 1)' and cites
some of its relevant provisions (*34*, p. 230). Martín invokes Fray
Luis de León's *La perfecta casada* (*33*, pp. 402–10), while Minett
quotes from Gerald Brenan's classic ethnological study, *South from
Granada*, dating from the 1920s and 30s:

> Even after marriage the women often remain cold,
> having been brought up through the influence of
> Catholicism to regard the sexual act as something
> unseemly which they must submit to patiently for the
> sake of keeping their husbands attached to them and of
> having children. And then these arrive. (*2*, p. 135 n11)

Helpful as all these are, they may be supplemented by
reference to the encyclical *Casti connubii* issued by Pope Pius XI at
the very end of 1930,[8] which would therefore have circulated in
Spain in 1931 — the very year Lorca is supposed to have had the
original idea for *Yerma*. Many of the doctrines contained in the
document are derived from St Augustine's *On Marriage and
Concupiscence*, which in turn draws a series of key ideas from Paul's
writings in First Corinthians, chapter 7, but the papal encyclical
serves well as an exemplar of contemporary, orthodox, prescriptive
teaching. Here marriage is described as being endowed with three

---

[8]Pope Pius XI, *Christian Marriage in View of the Present Condition, Needs,
Errors and Vices that Affect the Family and Society: Encyclical Letter of His
Holiness, Pope Pius XI*, reprinted from the text issued by the Vatican
Polyglot Press (1930) (Washington, DC: National Catholic Welfare
Conference, 1931), original text dated 31 December 1930 (p. 47).

primary goods or blessings, and the first among these is the procreation and bringing-up of children (pp. 6–9). The other two are a conjugal union that implies mutual fidelity, faith, honour and unity (that is to say, chastity, in the sense of the monogamous exclusivity of the two spouses to one another and their pure and mutual love for one another) (pp. 4–6, 9–12), and the sacrament of marriage, 'by which is denoted both the indissolubility of the bond and the raising and hallowing of the contract by Christ Himself' (pp. 3, 6, 12–15). There are also two secondary benefits, namely mutual aid between the spouses, both material and spiritual, and the legitimate relief of concupiscence (p. 21). Beyond these five principles, the encyclical also contains a number of other assertions and distinctions worthy of note. Within marriage, there is no doubt as to the primacy of the husband and subjection of the wife, though this unequal relationship is tempered by the latter's 'most noble office as wife and mother and companion', and the recommendation that 'as he occupies the chief place in ruling, so she may and ought to claim for herself the chief place in love' (p. 11). Furthermore, the encyclical states that 'it is wrong to leave a wife that is sterile in order to take another by whom children may be had. Anyone doing this is guilty of adultery' (p. 14), and, lastly, that 'nor are those considered as acting against nature who in the married state use their right [to sexual intercourse] in the proper manner although on account of natural reasons either of time or of certain defects, new life cannot be brought forth' (p. 21).

Turning back to *Yerma*, we can appreciate that the women in the play adopt a range of attitudes towards this set of ideas that reflect combinations of different priorities in different measures. Yerma herself focusses narrowly and almost exclusively on procreation (and upbringing) — in her own words 'la cría y el cuido de la cría' (79), though of course she ends up in that category of wives from whom 'new life cannot be brought forth'. María clearly embodies the most balanced implementation of these teachings, in that she has a caring, faithful relationship with her husband, they are committed to the procreation (Act I, Scene i) and upbringing (Act II, Scene ii) of children, while María's description of their lovemaking (40–41) demonstrates that it conforms exactly to the notion of the legitimate relief of concupiscence within marriage. At the other end of the scale to Yerma, the most rebellious character in the play is the Muchacha 2ª, who flouts authority in at least two ways. She does not want to become a mother and is very pleased that she has not become pregnant, while at the same time she makes it patently clear that she was having regular sexual intercourse with her boyfriend before they were married, and that little has changed after the exchange of wedding vows:

> Bueno, y además…, una se casa en realidad mucho antes de ir a la iglesia. […] ¿Qué necesidad tiene mi marido de ser mi marido? Porque lo mismo hacíamos de novios que ahora. (54–55)

In fact, the topic of procreation — that is, the first of the primary blessings of matrimony — is treated in *Yerma* in all its facets and in some detail, from sexual relations to conception, pregnancy, childbirth and motherhood, and thence to its negative manifestation, childlessness. In terms of church teaching, there are actually more characters in the play who emphasize the relief of concupiscence over the goal of a chaste marriage. However, for the most part this preference is presented in positive terms, as more in accord with the exuberance of the surrounding natural world and also, on occasion, as connecting with a very different religious perspective, namely the pagan and pantheistic, which tends to celebrate human physicality and sensuality.

The Vieja, for instance, with her two husbands and fourteen offspring, has obviously enjoyed a long, sexually active, and pleasure-filled life, and is therefore quite close in spirit to the Muchacha 2ª, though in her case this has always been within the bounds of marriage. She readily admits that she prefers entertainment and diversion over hard work:

> Yo he sido una mujer de faldas en el aire,[9] he ido
> flechada a la tajada de melón, a la fiesta, a la torta de
> azúcar. Muchas veces me he asomado de madrugada a la
> puerta creyendo oír música de bandurrias que iba, que
> venía, pero era el aire. (48)

As for sex, she explains with only a hint of euphemism that 'yo me
he puesto boca arriba y he comenzado a cantar' (49), and on
questioning Yerma further she realizes that Yerma's experiences
have been totally different from her own:

> Todo lo contrario que yo. [...] Los hombres tienen que
> gustar, muchacha. Han de deshacernos las trenzas y
> darnos de beber agua con su misma boca. Así corre el
> mundo. (50)

Likewise, part of the Lavanderas' song is a veritable paean to joyful
and uninhibited sexual activity, expressed in the most transparent of
imagery:

> LAVANDERA 5ª: Dime si tu marido
>   guarda semilla
>   para que el agua cante
>   por tu camisa.
>
> [...]
>
> LAVANDERA 2ª: Por el monte ya llega
>   mi marido a comer.
>   Él me trae una rosa
>   y yo le doy tres.
>
> LAVANDERA 5ª: Por el llano ya vino
>   mi marido a cenar.
>   Las brasas que me entrega

---

[9]The primary implication of this phrase is that she liked to dance a lot,
swirling her skirts in the air, but it could also allude to sexual encounters.

cubro con arrayán.

LAVANDERA 4ª: Por el aire ya viene
mi marido a dormir.
Yo alhelíes rojos
y él rojo alhelí. (71–72)

A similar atmosphere of unrestrained eroticism predominates in Act III, Scene ii. The *romería* depicted here is held every October (54), and as most *romerías* it is a popular festival. The participants, inhabitants of the surrounding area, would travel on foot, on horseback, by cart or by wagon following one or more established routes to the holy site, thereby forming a kind of pilgrimage or procession. Upon arrival, a variety of rites and celebrations would be held in the chapel and its immediate environs, seeking the blessing or help of the local saint.[10] But the theoretically Christian festivities at the shrine serve here as a pretext for carousing and all manner of taboo-breaking sexual activity, as was indeed often the case with *romerías*. The tone and content of the dance and song of the Macho and Hembra masks pick up that of the Lavanderas:

MACHO: Si tú vienes a la romería
a pedir que tu vientre se abra,
no te pongas un velo de luto,
sino dulce camisa de holanda.
Vete sola detrás de los muros,
donde están las higueras cerradas,
y soporta mi cuerpo de tierra
hasta el blanco gemido del alba.

[...]

HOMBRE 1º: ¡Dale ya con el cuerno!

---

[10]For more on *romerías*, see Allen Josephs, *White Wall of Spain: The Mysteries of Andalusian Culture* (Ames, IA: Iowa State University Press, 1983), pp. 119, 129. See chapter 10 for more information on the specific *romería* on which Lorca's depiction is modelled.

[…]

NIÑO: Dale ya con el aire.

HOMBRE 2°: Dale ya con la rama. (114–15)

María and the Muchacha 1ª are the only characters present to voice their disapproval, and in doing so they actually offer further details of the variety of goings-on:

MUCHACHA 1ª: El año pasado, cuando se hizo oscuro, unos mozos atenazaron con sus manos los pechos de mi hermana.

MARÍA: En cuatro leguas a la redonda no se oyen más que palabras terribles.

MUCHACHA 1ª: Más de cuarenta toneles de vino he visto en las espaldas de la ermita.

MARÍA: Un río de hombre solos baja por esas sierras. (109–10)

In stark contrast, the Vieja is cynically pragmatic about what really happens at the *romería*:

Venís a pedir hijos al Santo y resulta que cada año vienen más hombres solos a esta romería. ¿Qué es lo que pasa? (*Ríe.*) (108)

Aquí vienen las mujeres a conocer hombres nuevos y el Santo hace el milagro. (118)

Indeed, she has come to find a woman for one of her sons, and suggests to Yerma in a matter-of-fact tone that she simply abandon Juan and come to live with them (118).

If sex is referred to and celebrated quite frequently, people are generally rather more reluctant to talk openly about the topics of conception and pregnancy, and on the relatively rare occasions on which they do, they tend to express themselves in vague, poetic or metaphorical language. Thus María offers that 'a mí me parece que mi niño es un palomo de lumbre que él [mi marido] me deslizó por la oreja' (41), and of the experience of discovering that she was pregnant:

> MARÍA: ¿No has tenido nunca un pájaro vivo apretado en la mano?
>
> YERMA: Sí.
>
> MARÍA: Pues lo mismo…, pero por dentro de la sangre. (39)

The Vieja tells Yerma that 'yo no sé nada. [...] Los hijos llegan como el agua' (49), and later announces enigmatically that 'para tener un hijo ha sido necesario que se junte el cielo con la tierra' (117). Again it is the Lavanderas who are more explicit in their allusions to conception:

> LAVANDERA 3ª: Hay que juntar flor con flor
> cuando el verano seca la sangre al
> segador.
>
> LAVANDERA 4ª: Y abrir el vientre a pájaros sin
> sueño
> cuando a la puerta llama
> tembloroso el invierno.
>
> LAVANDERA 1ª: Hay que gemir en la sábana.
>
> LAVANDERA 4ª: ¡Y hay que cantar!
>
> LAVANDERA 5ª: Cuando el hombre nos trae
> la corona y el pan.
>
> LAVANDERA 4ª: Porque los brazos se enlazan. (72)

A little later, following the most natural of logics, the Lavanderas' song moves on to the topic of pregnancy:

LAVANDERA 6ª (*Apareciendo en lo alto del torrente.*):
　　　　　　　　　Para que un niño funda
　　　　　　　　　yertos vidrios del alba.

LAVANDERA 4ª:　　Y nuestro cuerpo tiene
　　　　　　　　　ramas furiosas de coral.

[…]

LAVANDERA 1ª:　　Un niño pequeño, un niño.
[…]

LAVANDERA 3ª:　　Un niño que gime, un hijo.
[…]

LAVANDERA 5ª:　　¡Alegría, alegría, alegría
　　　　　　　　　del vientre redondo bajo la camisa!

LAVANDERA 2ª:　　¡Alegría, alegría, alegría,
　　　　　　　　　ombligo, cáliz tierno de maravilla!
　　　　　　　　　(73–74)

A more modest range of viewpoints about childbirth and motherhood is also offered in the play. A description of giving birth is an integral part of Dolores's account of what supposedly happened with the last woman whom she helped conceive:

DOLORES: La última vez hice la oración con una mujer mendicante, que estaba seca más tiempo que tú, y se le endulzó el vientre de manera tan hermosa que tuvo dos criaturas ahí abajo, en el río, porque no le daba tiempo a llegar a las casas, y ella misma las trajo en un pañal para que yo las arreglase.

YERMA: ¿Y pudo venir andando desde el río?

DOLORES: Vino. Con los zapatos y las enaguas empapadas en sangre…, pero con la cara reluciente.

YERMA: ¿Y no le pasó nada?

DOLORES: ¿Qué le iba a pasar? Dios es Dios.

YERMA: Naturalmente. No le podía pasar nada, sino
agarrar las criaturas y lavarlas con agua viva. Los
animales los lamen, ¿verdad? (96)

María has recently discovered that she is pregnant, and although
pleased she is also disconcerted and a little intimidated by the
prospect of motherhood. Muchacha 1ª, the young woman who
already has a child, is depicted — at least to Yerma's way of
thinking — as rather neglectful. She has had to take food to her
husband in the fields, leaving the baby at home unattended. Yerma
checks with her that there are no pigs in the house and that the door
was locked; only mildly reassured, she insists that children cannot be
left alone and are highly vulnerable (53–54). The Muchacha 2ª,
married but childless, presents, as we have noted, a very different
attitude: she is content not to have any children and does not really
want to have any (*48*, p. 24). She got married not in order to be able
to have children but rather because her parents insisted; now her
mother is anxious for her to get pregnant, but she herself is in no
rush whatsoever (54–55). Yerma, of course, offers yet another
perspective (see chapter 6): she envies both María and the Muchacha
1ª, she implies she would be a better, more solicitous mother than the
latter, while she disagrees radically with the Muchacha 2ª's position.
Each of these secondary female characters, then, serves as a foil that
helps to locate Yerma more precisely.

Childlessness is the other side of the coin of procreation, and
there is a whole spectrum of opinions expressed in the play
concerning the condition. Yerma herself is particularly severe in this
regard: 'La mujer del campo que no da hijos es inútil como un
manojo de espinos, ¡y hasta mala!' (84). María consoles Yerma with
the anecdote that 'Una hermana de mi madre lo tuvo a los catorce
años [de su boda], ¡y si vieras qué hermosura de niño!' (42). The
Vieja first offers the rather woolly speculation that since Yerma feels
no physical attraction for Juan 'quizá por eso no hayas parido a
tiempo' (50), but goes on to refer more pointedly to 'los hombres de
simiente podrida que encharcan la alegría de los campos' (52). The
Lavanderas' song laments the woeful lot of the childless woman:

'LAVANDERA 2ª: ¡Ay de la casada seca! / ¡Ay de la que tiene los pechos de arena!' (71). In conversation the Lavandera 1ª asserts that the fault lies with Juan, that Yerma is not responsible for her infertility, and indeed that there would be no problem, no friction, and hence no fuel for gossip, if only she had children (65, 67, 68). Two of the others, however, are much more critical and judgemental:

> LAVANDERA 4ª: Le cuesta trabajo estar en su casa.

> LAVANDERA 5ª: Estas machorras[11] son así. Cuando podían estar haciendo encajes o confituras de manzanas, les gusta subirse al tejado y andar descalzas por esos ríos.
> [...]

> LAVANDERA 4ª: Tiene hijos la que quiere tenerlos. Es que las regalonas, las flojas, las endulzadas, no son a propósito para llevar el vientre arrugado. (65–66)

Dolores is also broadly sympathetic, in that she tries to help Yerma conceive and claims to have helped many other women in the past, at least some of them successfully:

> Muchas veces yo he hecho estas oraciones en el cementerio con mujeres que ansiaban crías… (95)

> La última vez hice la oración con una mujer mendicante, que estaba seca más tiempo que tú… (96)

But again others are less supportive. The Vieja 1ª who assists Dolores is more neutral, understanding but at the same time more resigned and fatalistic:

> Está bien que una casada quiera hijos, pero si no los tiene, ¿por qué ese ansia de ellos? [...] No te critico. Ya has visto cómo he ayudado a los rezos. (97)

---

[11]A rather technical term meaning a sterile woman.

> Eres demasiado joven para oír consejo. Pero, mientras
> esperas la gracia de Dios, debes ampararte en el amor de
> tu marido. (98)

María too implies a kind of passive acceptance in her slightly cryptic remark that 'tiene hijos la que los tiene que tener' (109). Finally, it is no coincidence that the local saint (never named) is believed to be endowed with special powers to remedy the affliction of barrenness. Evidently many women participate in the yearly *romería* in which they travel to the chapel up in the mountains and make offerings to the saint in his shrine (107), and as we have seen some of them while there avail themselves of the opportunity for extra-marital sexual encounters that may result in pregnancy.

Sexual and marital issues are also at the root of other powerful forces that operate within this society. For instance, while the *romería* seems to offer a brief period of special, sanctioned licence, when the usual rules are not enforced or people turn a blind eye (a little like the Saturnalia or Carnival), under normal circumstances the fidelity of the wife — and perhaps above all the appearance of her fidelity — is crucially important. Adultery, even the merest suspicion of adultery, is a grievous offence. Ideally, a married woman should not even look at another man: 'LAVANDERA 4ª: Hay una cosa en el mundo que es la mirada. Mi madre lo decía. No es lo mismo una mujer mirando a unas rosas que una mujer mirando a los muslos de un hombre' (67). If a woman stays busy indoors at home — as mandated by her traditional sex-role — this brings the added advantage that she is much less likely to become the target for gossip. Hence these exchanges between Juan and Yerma:

> YERMA: Nunca salgo.
>
> JUAN: Estás mejor aquí.
>
> YERMA: Sí.
>
> JUAN: La calle es para la gente desocupada.
>
> YERMA (*Sombría.*): Claro. (35–36)

and later: 'JUAN: Tú sales demasiado' (78); 'JUAN: Por eso quiero ver cerrada esa puerta y cada persona en su casa [...] cierras la boca y piensas que eres una mujer casada' (81). Even when the women must take food for the midday meal to the men working in the fields (another typically female task) (46–47, 53), they should not linger en route: 'JUAN: ¿Qué haces todavía aquí? YERMA: Hablaba. [...] JUAN: Debías estar en casa' (61).

The notion of honour is inextricably linked with these views of marriage, fidelity and the role and place of woman in society. Honour is construed both as an internal and an external force, as integrity — i.e. a personal code of conduct, and as reputation — i.e. what other people think of you, whether they consider you an honourable person or not, though the external, socially ratified version tends to predominate in the play (*18*, pp. 24–26). Honour as reputation is highly prized and easily lost, or at least diminished, as it depends not only on what you actually do or do not do, but also on what other people think you have done or not done, and whether they deem these actions acceptable or not. Although every individual in theory has honour (reputation) and can see it damaged, honour becomes most important within marriage and a family. Following an age-old belief common all around the Mediterranean, a married man's honour is located primarily in his wife's untarnished reputation; if there is the slightest shadow of a doubt of infidelity on her part, it reflects badly on him. Hence as Juan pithily puts it: 'Mi vida está en el campo, pero mi honra está aquí. Y mi honra es también vuestra' (76–77); 'las familias tienen honra y la honra es una carga que se lleva entre todos' (81). Juan therefore considers himself to possess honour, as does both the family from which he descends and the new family unit he has created in marrying Yerma. We can see this in Juan's location of honour: 'que está oscura y débil en los mismos caños de la sangre' (81), in Yerma's recrimination that: 'te figuras tú y tu gente que sois vosotros los únicos que guardáis honra' (103), and in Juan's frequent concerns about his reputation in the village in the light of Yerma's behaviour: 'YERMA: En nada te he faltado. JUAN: No me gusta que la gente me señale' (81). Indeed, as he becomes more annoyed by what he considers to be erratic actions on the part of Yerma, he finds himself obliged by the honour code to keep silent: 'Si pudiera dar voces, levantaría a todo el pueblo, para que viera dónde iba la honra de mi casa; pero he de ahogarlo todo y callarme porque eres mi mujer' (101).

Yerma, too, considers herself a woman of honour and from a family of honour, though in personal terms her notion of honour has a lot more to do with integrity. Despite Juan's accusations and complaints, she firmly believes that nothing she does strays from the path of rectitude: 'En nada te ofendo' (78), and that her honour is untarnished: 'esta limpieza que me cubre' (102). Even at the very end of the play, she still finds it hard to believe that Juan could even suspect her of infidelity: '¿Te figuras que puedo conocer otro hombre? ¿Dónde pones mi honra?' (118). But above all for Yerma, honour is inextricably wrapped up with her sense of family and tradition, and the word which she repeatedly uses for this latter concept is the highly charged term 'casta' (chapter 2). Referring to gossipy villagers, Yerma comments: 'Creen que me puede gustar otro hombre y no saben que, aunque me gustara, lo primero de mi casta es la honradez' (86); in conversation with Dolores Yerma asserts that she will stay with Juan come what may, 'por honra y por casta' (99); and when Juan accuses her, she rebukes him thus: 'no sabes que mi casta no ha tenido nunca nada que ocultar' (103).

Other characters have things to say about honour also. When Yerma pushes the Vieja for information on how she conceived and had children, the Vieja is reluctant to talk about such matters as they border on the taboo. All of the issues involved are delicate and volatile: sex, the possible infertility of the man or the woman. So the Vieja prefers to avoid the risk involved: 'No me hagas hablar más. No quiero hablarte más. Son asuntos de honra y yo no quemo la honra de nadie' (51). In a different key, honour is for the Lavanderas not a birthright but rather something that is earned, and earned primarily through socially acceptable behaviour:

LAVANDERA 5ª: La que quiera honra, que la gane.

LAVANDERA 4ª: Yo planté un tomillo,
                            yo lo vi crecer.
                            El que quiera honra,
                            que se porte bien. (64)

Another factor which controls almost all women's behaviour, be they married or unmarried, is a sense of shame — *vergüenza*, that is, an acute version of modesty, reserve and decency, inculcated from an early age. Thus María feels embarrassed at the very news that she is pregnant (40), and Yerma never acted on the feelings that she experienced with Víctor when she was younger because she also was too bashful (50). Many important things — like the facts of life — cannot be talked about because of this inhibition:

YERMA (*Triste.*): Las muchachas que se crían en el campo, como yo, tienen cerradas todas las puertas. Todo se vuelven medias palabras, gestos, porque todas estas cosas dicen que no se pueden saber. (51)

Shame therefore constitutes a strong social force that both regulates and restricts. For those for whom shame does not function as a powerful, internalized guide to sanctioned and unsanctioned behaviours, there is of course the further factor of appearances and gossip. On the other hand, and quite revealingly, there is very little mention in the play of the notion of conscience or of religious teaching on human conduct (and contravention of that teaching). It is interesting to note that the two times sin is referred to, it is more in the sense of breaking a social taboo than a theological rule: 'LAVANDERA 1ª: Hablar no es pecado' (66); 'YERMA: Hablar con la gente no es pecado. JUAN: Pero puede parecerlo' (81).

If shame functions, as it were, from within individuals, then gossip — and the danger of becoming a subject of gossip — functions from without, as an equally powerful inducement to normative, conformist behaviour. The village is small enough for everyone to know everyone else's business, and for few actions to go unobserved by someone. One's reputation, then, is immediately threatened when one becomes the topic of talk, and fear of *el qué dirán* is nearly ubiquitous. The Lavanderas scene is of course the purest incarnation of this phenomenon; while the women toil at the riverbank, they pass the time and add a little spice to their humdrum lives by engaging in — sometimes salacious — gossip. Thus, with a particularly nice irony, the act of washing clothes is accompanied by the airing of the village's 'dirty laundry' (*1*, pp. 19–20). Only Lavandera 1ª does not want to be a part of it, but others justify the activity:

> LAVANDERA 1ª: A mí no me gusta hablar.
>
> LAVANDERA 3ª: Pero aquí se habla.
>
> LAVANDERA 4ª: Y no hay mal en ello. (63–64)

Gossip has a tendency to take on a life of its own, for the stories to become embelished on each successive retelling, and Lavandera 1ª constantly questions and rebuts the dubious assertions that the others blithely make: 'Pero es que nunca se sabe nada' (64); '¿Pero se puede saber lo que ha ocurrido?' (65); '¿Quién eres tú para decir estas cosas?' (65); 'Pero ¿vosotras la habéis visto con otro?' (66); '¡Siempre las gentes!' (66); 'Hablar no es pecado' (66); '¡Eso es mentira!' (67); all of which leads her to conclude that: 'Con una aguja de hacer calceta ensartaría yo las lenguas murmuradoras' (68). What it all boils down to is this: they know that despite having been married for over three years Yerma is still childless, the most recent tidbit of news is that Juan has brought in the two Cuñadas to live with them and Yerma has reacted badly to their arrival, and unspecified 'other people' have purportedly observed Yerma on two occasions talking with another man, whom they are reluctant to identify by name but who is presumably Víctor (64–67). Everything else is supposition, innuendo and embroidery, which are in plentiful supply.

Juan and Yerma have several arguments about village gossip. Juan is entirely conventional in this regard: he does not want his reputation threatened and he does not want to know that he is the subject of other villagers' whispered exchanges. He recognizes that it is above all a question of appearances, and while during most of the course of the play he has no doubts about Yerma's actual behaviour, nonetheless he subscribes to the majority viewpoint that appearances must be kept up at all costs:

> JUAN: Está bien. Así darás que hablar a las gentes.
>
> YERMA (*Fuerte.*): Juan, ¿qué piensas?
>
> JUAN: No lo digo por ti, lo digo por las gentes. (61)

> JUAN: No me gusta que la gente me señale. Por eso
> quiero ver cerrada esa puerta y cada persona en su casa.
>
> YERMA: Hablar con la gente no es pecado.
>
> JUAN: Pero puede parecerlo. (81)

However, as the years pass and Yerma begins to act, to his mind, more strangely and scandalously, he loses his patience and seriously questions Yerma's probity, for, after all, an adulterous but barren wife has no need of contraceptives:

> JUAN: ¿Qué haces en este sitio?
> […]
>
> JUAN: Y yo no puedo más. Porque se necesita ser de
> bronce para ver a tu lado una mujer que […] se sale de
> noche fuera de su casa, ¿en busca de qué? ¡Dime!,
> ¿buscando qué? Las calles están llenas de machos. En las
> calles no hay flores que cortar.
>
> YERMA: […] guárdate de poner nombre de varón sobre
> mis pechos.
>
> JUAN: No soy yo quien lo pone; lo pones tú con tu
> conducta y el pueblo lo empieza a decir. Lo empieza a
> decir claramente. Cuando llego a un corro, todos callan;
> cuando voy a pesar la harina, todos callan; y hasta de

noche en el campo, cuando despierto a medianoche, me
parece que también se callan las ramas de los árboles.
[...]

JUAN: Ni yo sé lo que busca una mujer a todas horas
fuera de su tejado. (101–03)

At the end of this scene of confrontation at Dolores's house the need
to cover up, to hide and be silent is vividly brought home as the
village begins to stir at daybreak and there are passers-by outside in
the street: 'JUAN: Calla. Vamos.'; 'JUAN: ¡Calla he dicho!
DOLORES: ¡Viene gente! Habla bajo'; 'DOLORES: Van a pasar
por aquí. JUAN: Silencio'; 'JUAN: Calla' (104–05).

In contrast, while Yerma is often in large part socially
conventional and conformist, one area where she is impatient and
resistant to the norm is in respect to appearances and gossip. In her
first conversation with Juan on the matter, she reacts angrily:
'¡Puñalada que le den a las gentes!' (61), and later, when Dolores
warns: '¡Viene gente! Habla bajo', Yerma replies: 'No me importa'
(105). Likewise she dismisses Juan and his sisters' suspicions as
'figuraciones. De gente que no tiene la conciencia tranquila' (86),
and in the showdown with Juan after he has surprised her at
Dolores's house, she will not allow herself to be, to her mind,
slandered:

No te dejo hablar ni una sola palabra. Ni una más. [...]
Anda, acércate a mí y huele mis vestidos; ¡acércate!, a
ver dónde encuentras un olor que no sea tuyo, que no sea
de tu cuerpo. [...] Haz conmigo lo que quieras, que soy
tu mujer, pero guárdate de poner nombre de varón sobre
mis pechos. (103)

Overall, the picture painted in this chapter would suggest a
society that is both repressed and repressive, and this is certainly the
case. But as we have also seen, the situation is more complex and
there are several notable exceptions to the dour, joyless lifestyle that
the Vieja attributes to Yerma's father and by extension her whole

family: 'Levantarse, sudar, comer unos panes y morirse. Ni más juego, ni más nada. Las ferias para otros. Criaturas de silencio' (47–48). Traditional teaching on licit sex within marriage contains a certain amount of room for manoeuvre, the constraints of fidelity, honour, shame and gossip are occasionally relaxed — as at the *romería*, and they can be bent or defied. This allows some of the villagers, like María and the Lavanderas, enough leeway to find personal and sexual satisfaction within the norm, while at least a few of the others, like the Vieja and Muchacha 2ª, are freer spirits who refuse to be bound completely by this rigid scheme of tenets imposed by society.

4. Plot and Structure

Yerma is conventionally structured in three acts, with each act split into two scenes ('cuadros').[12] Normally such a division would correspond, broadly speaking, to the well-known tripartite pattern of exposition, development and denouement, and this is substantially the case here, where exposition is achieved in Act I, Scene i ('el primer cuadro de la tragedia, donde se plantea de lleno el asunto' [137]), and the denouement — a surprise ending for those not familiar with the play — in Act III, Scene ii. But it is harder to see much real plot development in Act II, where the situation remains essentially the same and only changes by dint of getting worse and more tense (*6*, p. 132). Indeed, of all Lorca's full-length plays, *Yerma* is probably the one where fewest things actually happen; people talk a lot but do very little. The action is reduced to a bare minimum: Yerma and Juan live together, Juan farms, Yerma wants children but does not conceive, she waits, becoming more bitter, desperate and anguished as the years pass, she resorts to folk remedies and superstitious beliefs, and at the very end, in an outburst, strangles her husband to death. That is all. There are no subplots — unless one wants to stretch the category and count Yerma's relationship with Víctor as such; the focus remains on Yerma and her longings throughout. Lorca was well aware of what he had created — and not created. This may be one reason why he subtitled the play a 'poema trágico' and not a 'tragedia' or 'tragedia poética' — the term 'poema' implies a minimum of dramatic

---

[12]The division into 'cuadros' is determined essentially by location and the corresponding stage set; a 'cuadro' ends and another begins when the action moves somewhere else. Lorca dispenses with the further subdivision into 'escenas', which are marked by the entrance or exit of one or more characters within a given 'cuadro'.

development. Furthermore, in newspaper interviews he stated that 'lo
más interesante de mi drama es el proceso obsesivo de la mujer, que
habla igual desde que sale hasta que desaparece' (196) and he
insisted that:

No hay argumento en *Yerma*. (181)

— Què passa? *Yerma* no té argument. *Yerma* és un
caràcter que es va desenvolupant en el transcurs dels sis
quadres de que consta l'obra. […] Repeteixo que *Yerma*,
d'argument no en té. En molts moments, el públic li
semblarà que n'hi ha, pero és un petit engany… (183)

Benítez offers a rather different but nonetheless
complementary way of looking at how the play is put together
structurally (*10*). According to this critic, if one focusses on possible
remedies to Yerma's plight (see chapter 6 for a detailed discussion of
her predicament), then broadly speaking these can be said to fall into
three categories: her husband, other men, and the miraculous (*10*, p.
40). Yerma explores each of these possibilities in turn, with Juan,
with Víctor, and with Dolores (and in part María). Hence, in one
sense, all the solutions are exhausted by the end of Act III, Scene i,
which is the moment when Yerma exclaims '¡Está escrito[!]' and
'¡Ya está!' (106; *10*, pp. 40–43). The very last scene of the play
could therefore be described as recapitulatory, in that it revisits one
final time all three categories before ushering in the denouement: the
romería offers a similar mix of Christian and pagan as do the rites
supervised by Dolores in the cemetery (chapter 7), the Vieja's son
deputizes, as it were, for Víctor, while Juan reappears in the closing
pages (*10*, pp. 43–44).

Since the plot, such as it is, repeatedly directs emphasis on to
Yerma waiting, hoping and then increasingly despairing (chapter 7),
it is logical that the play should be carefully articulated in
chronological terms, and Lorca inserts several references to orient
the audience as to the progression of time. In Act I, Scene i, Yerma
and Juan have been married for two years, an initial reference to
'veinticuatro meses' (33) being refined later by Yerma, who has

evidently been counting the days, as 'dos años y veinte días' (41); in Act I, Scene ii another year has elapsed (47). There is no temporal indication for Act II, Scene i, though it would perhaps not be totally out of place to speculate that a further twelve months or so had passed, for in Act II, Scene ii Yerma and Juan have now been together for over five years (79). Another visual indicator is that María, who announced her pregnancy to Yerma in Act I, Scene i (38) now has 'un niño en brazos' (83) — he should be about two and a half years old. Breaking this year-by-year rhythm, Act III, Scene i takes place just a few hours after the preceding scene, Yerma having spent the intervening time with Dolores and the two Viejas in the cemetery. It is not entirely clear how much time elapses between Scenes i and ii in Act III, but María's comment that 'ella ha estado un mes sin levantarse de la silla' (109) may well provide the key, if we assume that Yerma's collapse occurred immediately after the end of Scene i. The action of the play on stage therefore covers a span of a little over three years.

There are also a variety of other chronological references. Yerma reminds Juan that 'cuando nos casamos eras otro' (32), and a few moments later she muses on the fact that 'tú y yo seguiremos aquí cada año' (33). María becomes pregnant five months after her wedding (38) and unthinkingly remarks to Yerma that 'de todas las novias de tu tiempo tú eres la única' (41), nearly completing the sentence before realizing how insensitive her observation is; Yerma counters with some half-hearted optimism: 'claro que todavía es tiempo. Elena tardó tres años, y otras antiguas, del tiempo de mi madre, mucho más' (41). Muchacha 2ª gives her age as nineteen (55) and complains about her mother (Dolores) who is planning to take her on the *romería* later that year in October (54).

In addition to this broad temporal framework, many of the scenes are set at a particular time of day and/or in a particular season which, as is almost always the case with Lorca, have symbolic significance. Thus Act I, Scene i opens with 'una alegre luz de mañana de primavera' (31), both morning and spring being traditionally associated with hope, a new beginning, (re)birth. Act I, Scene ii is set towards the middle of the day, as the women are taking lunch to the men working in the olive groves. In Act II, Scene ii, dusk is falling (76) and they are preparing to have dinner; later 'la escena está en una suave penumbra' (89), through the doorway of the house can be seen 'la última luz de la tarde' (90), near the end of the scene 'la escena está casi a oscuras' (93), and finally 'la escena está oscurísima' (94). It is as if with Víctor's departure the last flicker of light, associated with hope, is extinguished. As Yerma spends the intervening hours in the cemetery, Act III, Scene i starts just as dawn is beginning to break (95); Yerma had planned to return home under the cover of darkness, but she has delayed too long, and Vieja 1ª warns her of the coming light of day (100). Finally, we know that the festivities at the chapel in honour of the local saint take place in October; a little way into the action of Act III, Scene ii 'empieza el anochecer' (110), later 'está muy anochecido' (112), while the opening song looks forward to midnight: 'Te desnudaré, / casada y romera, / cuando en lo oscuro las doce den' (107). Overall, the action therefore moves from morning to night, and from spring to autumn.

Chronological markers, then, are evidently very important, in the plot, in how the play is structured, and in symbolic implications. But location also plays a significant role. Basically the scenes create an alternating counterpoint (AB — BA — AB) between inside (A) and outside (B), between being within a building and being outside in the open air (*2*, p. 25; *3*, pp. 32–33). The pattern is as follows: I-i inside Yerma's house; I-ii a path or road in the countryside, near the olive groves; II-i a riverbank near the village; II-ii inside Yerma's house; III-i inside Dolores's house; III-ii a mountainside, in the area immediately surrounding the chapel and shrine of a local saint. Lorca was well aware of the oppositional patterning that he had created, and commented in an interview on the effects he sought to create:

Seis cuadros; los que necesité hacer. Que no pienso yo puedan ponerse límites de medida a una concepción dramática. De estos cuadros, tres, los que corresponden a los interiores, tienen un dramatismo reconcentrado, una emoción silenciosa, como reflejo plástico de un tormento espiritual; los otros tres, al recibir color y ambiente

natural, ponen luminarias de luz en el tono oscuro de la
tragedia. (160)

Within these temporal and spatial coordinates we encounter
the characters who are on stage in the course of the six scenes. Even
the most cursory examination reveals that during much of the play
the preferred dramatic model is the simple situation of Yerma
engaged in conversation with one other individual (*1*, p. 27). Thus
Act I, Scene i can be broken down into the following units or
subdivisions ('escenas' in the sense defined above): the short, mimed
opening dream sequence, Yerma with Juan, Yerma briefly alone,
Yerma with María, Yerma very briefly alone, Yerma with Víctor,
Yerma briefly alone. Act I, Scene ii is quite similar: Yerma with the
Vieja, Yerma with Muchacha 1ª and Muchacha 2ª, Yerma with
Muchacha 2ª, Yerma with Víctor, Yerma with Juan.[13] In Act I,
Scene i Lorca leaves brief pauses between one character's exit and
the next one's entrance, but in Act I, Scene ii characters make their
entrance very much on the heels of the previous one's exit. This very
basic compositional structure is only rendered a little more
sophisticated in I–ii when Muchacha 1ª exits but Yerma continues
the conversation with Muchacha 2ª, and when Juan very briefly
overlaps with Víctor on stage.

In Act II, Scene i the group of six Lavanderas, later joined by
the two Cuñadas, therefore creates a strong contrast by dint of the
high number of characters on stage simultaneously. Their gossipy,
free-flowing conversation is punctuated by worksongs whose content
also relates to Yerma and Juan (see chapters 3 and 6). Act II, Scene ii
largely reverts to the original model, though the presence now of the
two sisters-in-law means that sometimes there are four people on
stage rather than two. The segmentation is as follows: Yerma with
Juan (during which the Cuñadas silently come and go), Yerma
briefly alone, Yerma with María (and the small child in arms),
Yerma with Muchacha 2ª, Yerma with Víctor, Yerma with Víctor

---

[13]Muchacha 1ª's exit is not marked in the stage directions but can be
inferred from the dialogue (54).

and Juan, and the brief close where Juan goes off with Víctor, Yerma leaves with Muchacha 2ª, and the two Cuñadas come out and call for Yerma. Minor subtleties here include the fact that Yerma is not on stage at the very opening of the scene, the momentary appearance of one of the sisters-in-law during Yerma's dialogue with María (86), a minor overlap of Víctor's entrance and Muchacha 2ª's exit, and the rather more complex comings and goings in the last pages of the act.

In Act III, Scene i, Yerma and Dolores are the primary interlocutors; Vieja 1ª does contribute a little to the conversation, but Vieja 2ª only has one line (95). Towards the end of the scene, with the arrival of Juan and the Cuñadas, there are now seven characters on stage, but the dialogue is limited to an extended exchange between Yerma and Juan with occasional punctuations from Dolores. The closing scene is of course quite different, with various groups of people moving around the stage. At one moment or another the audience would see Yerma, the Vieja, six Mujeres, María, Muchacha 1ª, seven Muchachas, the Macho and Hembra, several Niños, two Hombres, and Juan, a total of some twenty-five characters. Obviously the exact figures are not that important — rather Lorca is interested in creating the kaleidoscopic effect of large numbers of poeple moving around in groups on a conventionally sized stage, and never is everyone on stage simultaneously, but the overall impression is quite different (with the partial exception of the Lavanderas' scene) from that offered by the rest of the play. Furthermore, the scene is constructed differently, with much shorter and more fluid units or segments. Yerma, the Vieja and Mujeres 1ª and 2ª talk briefly then exit; María talks with Muchacha 1ª then Yerma re-enters with six Mujeres (it seems that María and Muchacha 1ª stay on stage). After they all leave, the central set piece of the scene, the performance of the two masks, Macho and Hembra, begins. Groups of Muchachas, in two and threes and trailing large ribbons, herald the appearance of Macho and Hembra; also on scene are the Niños and Hombres 1º and 2º. After the dance and song they all leave, and two more familiar segments follow. First Yerma is with the Vieja, and the moment the latter leaves, Juan appears (he has been eavesdropping on their conversation), and their final dialogue leads to the climactic act with which the play ends, leaving Yerma alone on stage with her husband's lifeless body while 'acude un grupo que queda al fondo' (124).

Besides revealing how each of the play's scenes is put together and demonstrating the relatively simple dramatic techniques at work, this kind of analysis also underlines one other feature: how much of the time Yerma is actually on stage. More than any other of Lorca's protagonists, she dominates the play in terms of her physical presence throughout. Leaving aside for a moment Act II, Scene i (the Lavanderas), Yerma is absent only at the very beginning and very end of Act II, Scene ii, and for two segments of Act III, Scene ii; a rough calculation puts her on stage for almost 80% of the play's total running time (*1*, p. 26). Going hand in hand with this feature is Yerma's centrality with regard to the other characters: they are articulated around her and their appearance in the play is justified dramatically in terms of their connection with her. Thus Juan is her husband, Víctor a childhood friend, the Cuñadas her sisters-in-law, the Vieja an acquaintance, María a friend, Muchachas 1ª and 2ª acquaintances, and Dolores an acquaintance. The only characters not to have a direct link with her are the Lavanderas from the village and the celebrants of the festivities at the shrine.

The text is written in a mixture of prose and verse. The characters converse in a prose that is relatively plausible in their mouths, though inevitably, upon closer analysis, we find it to be laden with metaphors and symbols (see chapter 5). Although prose predominates throughout, there are nonetheless several passages written in poetry, and only one out of the six scenes, Act III, Scene i, is completely devoid of verse. It is not always entirely clear if, in performance, these sections of poetry are to be recited or sung, with or without music.

The play opens with a sung lullaby — 'A la nana, nana, nana' (31), and a little later Yerma sings '¿De dónde vienes, amor, mi niño' (36–37), six lines of which are repeated as a reprise at the very

end of the scene (45).[14] In Act I, Scene ii, Víctor's shepherd's song,
'¿Por qué duermes solo, pastor?' is echoed by Yerma (56–57; music
204). The next scene with the Lavanderas is a complex mix of prose,
poetry and song. Opening with the *seguidilla* 'En el arroyo claro'
(63; music 205), the (prose) conversation is immediately interrupted
by another sung *copla*, 'Yo planté un tomillo' (64).[15] Prose dialogue
continues (64–70) until the *seguidilla* returns in a much more
extended form (70–72). But the song itself is punctuated by two lines
of verse: 'LAVANDERA 2ª: ¡Ay de la casada seca! / ¡Ay de la que
tiene los pechos de arena!' (71), and the entire conversation that
follows the song is also conducted in similar verse (72–74). The
metrical scheme is far from simple, involving four subdivisions of
the conversation, the first and third employing even line-lengths (6,
8, 12 and 14 syllables), the second and fourth odd line-lengths (7, 9
and 13 syllables). Assonance is used throughout; independent
assonating couplets predominate in the first section, but then the
scheme becomes less regular and more complex in the subsequent
sections. A final reprise of the *seguidilla* rounds off the scene (75).
Yerma's monologue poem or song '¡Ay, qué prado de pena!'
(82–83) covers a transitional point in Act II, Scene ii. The last scene
— like the Lavanderas' — contains prose, poetry and song. It opens
with song: '(*Canto a telón corrido.*) No te pude ver' (107; music
206), followed by prose dialogue (108–10). Then Yerma enters with
the Mujeres, presumably chanting their verse prayer (110–11). Again
there is some metric variation here, with combinations of assonating
8- and 9-syllable lines bracketing Yerma's 8-syllable *romance* 'El
cielo tiene jardines' with assonance *i-a* in the even lines. Next, the
whole section involving the masks of Macho and Hembra is written

---

[14]The music for the lullaby is given in Hernández's edition, 203; at the end
of Yerma's sewing song there is the unequivocal stage direction 'YERMA
queda cantando' (37), though no music seems to have survived.

[15]The *seguidilla* is a very old verse form: typically, in a four-line stanza, the
first and third lines are six or seven syllables long, and the second and fourth
five syllables long, with assonance between the even line endings. *Copla* is a
broader term referring to a short verse composition intended to be sung,
usually with four lines of a variable syllable count (eight or fewer).

in verse; Macho and Hembra dance, accompanied by bells, but only at the very end is there a stage direction that indicates that the last four lines are to be sung, implying that all those that precede are — presumably — to be recited or intoned ritualistically. In metrical terms, this section can be broken down into five subdivisions, marked by even- and odd-syllable line lengths. The first subdivision is almost all 8-syllables, the next mainly 7-syllable (with some longer lines at the end), the next predominantly 10-syllables, the next almost all 7-syllables, with a final brief run of 8-syllables. The first four subdivisions are characterized by assonance *a-a* in alternating lines, and sometimes in successive lines; the fifth subdivision shifts to *i-a*, as it is a brief reprise of Yerma's poetic prayer. Thereafter the dialogue continues in prose until the final curtain (116–24). The interplay of sections of lines of even and odd syllable numbers here mirrors that found in Act II, Scene i, further linking the Lavanderas' scene with the *romería*.

5. Nature and Symbolism

Given the location of the action of the play, it follows that nature and the natural world form a backdrop against which we see the characters and their lives. And because this is a farming community, most of the references to nature come from the domain of agriculture. Oxen, sheep, lambs and dogs populate the landscape (32, 33, 36, 45, 69–70, 84), there are fields and meadows, olive groves and apple orchards, oaks and broom bushes (46, 52, 53, 57, 76, 77). The wheat thrives: 'LAVANDERA 4ª: Si los trigos verdes tuvieran cabeza, temblarían de verlos [rebaños] venir' (70); 'YERMA: …los trigos apuntan' (84); hedge mustard and thyme bloom (35, 64). The sun shines (31), springs and fountains gurgle (84), the wind blows (36, 73), and overall there is a suggestion of elemental rightness, of what the Vieja calls 'la alegría de los campos' (52).

Men and women, children and grandparents, live out their lives within this rural, natural world. Families, as we have seen, are very important here. Sexual pleasure is, according to the Vieja, what makes the world go round: 'Los hombres tienen que gustar, muchacha. […] Así corre el mundo' (50). The frequent references to conception, pregnancy, childbirth and motherhood have already been noted (chapter 3); at the other end of spectrum, Yerma alludes to 'los ancianos' and Muchacha 2ª to 'las viejas' and 'los viejos' (53, 55). The idea of successive generations leads obviously to that of inheritance, even though Juan is untypical in this regard: 'VÍCTOR: Quiere juntar dinero y lo juntará, pero ¿a quién lo va a dejar cuando se muera?' (45).

But the presentation of mankind, of human life and death, against the backdrop of nature points up one crucial dissimilarity within what might otherwise be a harmonious continuum. The vegetal world of Nature is seasonal and cyclical, the trees, shrubs and flowers come and go, the yearly crops — such as wheat — are harvested and some of the grains thus gathered provide the seed to be sown the following year. But human life is linear, with a beginning, middle and end, and while families can perpetuate themselves through successive generations, each individual never returns. Hence perhaps the acute sense of the brevity of life: 'VIEJA: Es lo que digo yo: las higueras, ¡cuánto duran!; las casas, ¡cuánto duran!; y sólo nosotras, las endemoniadas mujeres, nos hacemos polvo por cualquier cosa' (48), and the repulsive finality of death: 'DOLORES: Que mi lengua se llene de hormigas, como está la boca de los muertos, si alguna vez he mentido' (96). Revealingly, this double vision, of a nurturing, bountiful nature, and at the same time of a cruel, or at least indifferent, nature, was commented on by Lorca himself:

> Porque hay dos naturalezas para los seres humanos: la naturaleza que los sostiene, hermana y madre, y la naturaleza sorda, enemiga del hombre, arrollando a miles de criaturas que no están conformes con sus leyes. (198)

We may surmise, then, that the author wanted both perspectives to be present and perceptible in the play.

The strongly archetypal feel to the texture and experience of life is picked up too in the symbolism found in the language of *Yerma*. Almost all the symbols derive from the worlds of nature and agriculture, with the result that they are often coherent and meaningful both on the literal level of expression and on the figurative plane. The two dominant areas of symbolism involve water/dryness and the colour white (*13*). Since this is a farming community, and since — as noted in chapter 2 — irrigation is such a crucial factor, most of the images of water and dryness possess a strong resonance. Generally speaking, then, water is good and connotes the presence of the life force, while dryness is bad and connotes its absence; the only real exception is when water is stagnant or putrid, and hence negatively charged.

Sexual activity is described in terms of water, 'VIEJA: Han de deshacernos las trenzas y darnos de beber agua con su misma boca'

(50), as is conception, 'VIEJA: Los hijos llegan como el agua' (49); 'LAVANDERA 5ª: Dime si tu marido / guarda semilla / para que el agua cante / por tu camisa' (71); 'VIEJA (*Con sorna.*): ¿Habéis bebido ya el agua santa?' (108). Yerma imagines the beggar woman's birthing thus: 'No le podía pasar nada, sino agarrar las criaturas y lavarlas con agua viva' (96). The crowds of men who attend the *romería* in hopes of anonymous sexual encounters are seen by María in similar terms: 'Un río de hombres solos baja por esas sierras' (110). Fertility, then, is associated with water, so that the barren wife seeking a remedy to her condition is depicted, in the song of the Macho and Hembra, as bathing in a river:

> HEMBRA: En el río de la sierra
> la esposa triste se bañaba.
> Por el cuerpo le subían
> los caracoles del agua.
>
> [...]
>
> NIÑO: Mirad qué oscuro se pone
> el chorro de la montaña. (112–13)[16]

Likewise, the river is an appropriate *locus* for childbirth:

> DOLORES: La última vez hice la oración con una mujer
> mendicante [...] y se le endulzó el vientre de manera tan
> hermosa que tuvo dos criaturas ahí abajo, en el río,
> porque no le daba tiempo a llegar a las casas, y ella
> misma las trajo en un pañal para que yo las arreglase.
>
> YERMA: ¿Y pudo venir andando desde el río? (96)

---

[16]In traditional Spanish lyric, the river bank is often depicted as a site where lovers meet, and there are even compositions that refer to washing clothes: e.g. 'nasce una fonte frida, / donde lavo la mi camisa / y la de aquel que yo más quería'. In the passage just cited, the reference is to the *topos* of the 'baño de amor', where, typically, two lovers bathe together in the river (*28*, pp. 212–15). Likewise, the two horns on the head of the water-snail sticking out of his shell have clear phallic associations (*28*, p. 212).

Logically enough, infertility is expressed in terms of dryness and being withered or dried up: 'LAVANDERA 2ª: ¡Ay de la casada seca! / ¡Ay de la que tiene los pechos de arena!' (71); 'DOLORES: una mujer mendicante, que estaba seca más tiempo que tú' (96); 'VIEJA: una casada seca' (108); 'HOMBRE 2°: ¡Ay, con el vientre seco / y la color quebrada!' (113); 'HOMBRE 1°: ¡Ay, marchita de amores!' (113).

Yerma adopts this same vocabulary for herself. She describes her barren state as dry: '¿Por qué estoy yo seca?' (48), 'Yo soy como un campo seco donde caben arando mil pares de bueyes' (118) (note the explicit link here with agriculture), and, later, as withered, dried up, parched and shrivelled up:

> VIEJA (*Fuerte.*): Pues sigue así. Por tu gusto es. Como los cardos del secano, pinchosa, marchita.
>
> YERMA (*Fuerte.*): Marchita sí, ¡ya lo sé! ¡Marchita!
> (119)
>
> YERMA: ¡Marchita!
> [...]
> YERMA: Marchita, marchita, pero segura. Ahora sí que lo sé de cierto. [...] Con el cuerpo seco para siempre.
> (123–24)

Given that this is the case, it again follows that Yerma should refer to her longing for children as a thirst, a thirst she cannot quench: 'la que se muere de sed' (52); 'quiero beber agua y no hay vaso ni agua' (80); 'las mujeres, cuando tenéis hijos, no podéis pensar en las que no los tenemos [...] como el que nada en agua dulce no tiene idea de la sed' (84–85); 'Yo pienso que tengo sed y no tengo libertad' (97). Her fantasy of pregnancy is also expressed in identical terms: 'y nuestro vientre guarda tiernos hijos / como la nube lleva dulce lluvia' (83). When the Lavanderas impugn Yerma's domesticity, another connection is made:

LAVANDERA 5ª: Estas machorras son así. Cuando podían estar haciendo encajes o confituras de manzanas, les gusta subirse al tejado y andar descalzas por esos ríos. (65)

And when Yerma slips away from the watchful eyes of the two Cuñadas, it transpires that she has gone to the village fountain, with the implication that what 'fresh water' symbolizes is what is lacking in their household:

JUAN: ¿Dices que salió hace poco? (*La* HERMANA MAYOR *contesta con la cabeza.*) Debe estar en la fuente. […]

JUAN: (*Entra* YERMA *con dos cántaros. Queda parada en la puerta.*) ¿Vienes de la fuente?

YERMA: Para tener agua fresca en la comida. (76–77)

The only kind of water that Yerma dislikes is stagnant water, water that has lost its vital force, such as has been sitting in a well: 'De mí sé decir que he aborrecido el agua de estos pozos' (89).[17] As a result the well itself can acquire a strong negative symbolic charge, such as when Yerma laments the nature and direction of her life: 'Ahora que voy entrando en lo más oscuro del pozo' (105), and when she rejects out of hand the Vieja's invitation to go and live with her and her son: 'lo que tú me das es un pequeño vaso de agua de pozo' (118).

Given the coordinates of this symbolism as established in the previous quotations, it comes as no surprise that Juan is characterized as dry. In their opening exchange Yerma is trying to give Juan a glass of milk to drink, to build him up, but Juan sees no need: 'Cuando los hombres se quedan enjutos se ponen fuertes como

[17]As we know that the village has at least one river, and that water can also be got at a spring or fountain, likely in the village square, Yerma's language here is not really realistic but rather motivated by the figurative value of 'agua de estos pozos'.

el acero' (32). The standard translation for 'enjuto' is something like wiry, lean or even gaunt, but the adjective derives from *enjutar/enjugar* which means to dry out, to dry up, so where English puts the emphasis on a lack of fat (lean), Spanish stresses a lack of water ('enjuto'). This point is driven home by Yerma:

> A mí me gustaría que fueras al río y nadaras, y que te subieras al tejado cuando la lluvia cala nuestra vivienda. [...] tú cada vez más triste, más enjuto, como si crecieras al revés. (32–33)

and later explicitly repeated: 'VÍCTOR: Y tu marido más triste que tú. YERMA: Él sí. Tiene un carácter seco' (58). There is considerable irony, therefore, when Juan says that he has to stay out in the fields all night: by doing so, he will be avoiding sexual activity and possible conception, both associated with water, in order to irrigate and hence fertilize his fields. It is almost as if he had transferred his affection from his wife to his land: 'YERMA: ¿Te espero? JUAN: No. Estaré toda la noche regando. Viene poca agua, es mía hasta la salida del sol y tengo que defenderla de los ladrones' (62). Less flattering still is the Vieja's comment about 'los hombres de simiente podrida que encharcan la alegría de los campos' (52), among whom she unequivocally includes Juan. The image of the putrid puddle resounds with Yerma's of the stagnant wells, and in a way prepares the ground for Yerma's more complex utterance:

> VIEJA: Mira qué maldición ha venido a caer sobre tu hermosura.
>
> YERMA: Una maldición. Un charco de veneno sobre las espigas. (117)

Putrid water has evolved into (liquid) poison, which in turn is spilt on the ears of wheat; besides the further agricultural reference, the wheat symbolizes fertility, growth and the natural.

Víctor, on the other hand, is closely connected with water. One of the youthful episodes when Yerma felt something special with

Víctor occurs when he helped her jump over an irrigation channel: 'Otra vez, el mismo Víctor, teniendo yo catorce años (él era un zagalón), me cogió en sus brazos para saltar una acequia y me entró un temblor que me sonaron los dientes' (50), and as a shepherd he is in charge of flocks, which are figuratively evoked as 'una inundación de lana' (70). Later when he enters singing (see the section below on the symbolism of song), his voice is much admired by Yerma: 'Y qué voz tan pujante. Parece un chorro de agua que te llena toda la boca' (58). If children were conceived the way María and the Vieja imagine it — 'la noche que nos casamos [mi marido] me lo decía constantemente con su boca puesta en mi mejilla, tanto que a mí me parece que mi niño es un palomo de lumbre que él me deslizó por la oreja' (41), 'los hombres [...] han de [...] darnos de beber agua con su misma boca' (50), 'los hijos llegan como el agua' (49) — by the terms of Yerma's passionate description, it almost seems as if Víctor could impregnate her just by singing and being heard by Yerma.

Finally, Yerma sometimes uses water imagery in a more extended, more abstract sense, though inevitably this always resonates with the basic symbolism just reviewed. Water now is opposed to stone (rather than to dryness). Thus in Yerma's first conversation with Juan, she declares:

> No. No me repitas lo que dicen. Yo veo por mis ojos que eso no puede ser... A fuerza de caer la lluvia sobre las piedras éstas se ablandan y hacen crecer jaramagos, que las gentes dicen que no sirven para nada. Los jaramagos no sirven para nada, pero yo bien los veo mover sus flores amarillas en el aire. (35)

Casting herself as rock, she draws hope regarding her infertility from the observation that rain can make flowers (hedge mustard) grow and bloom in the most inhospitable of places. She also rejects conventional wisdom, both about sterility and conception and about the flowers themselves, which thrive and are visually attractive despite their perceived lack of utility. Almost identical imagery returns in a subsequent conversation with Juan, needless to say on the same topic, where the meaning now is quite transparent:

JUAN: ...te empeñas en meter la cabeza por una roca.

YERMA: Roca que es una infamia que sea roca, porque debía ser un canasto de flores y agua dulce. (80)

Metaphorically, this is broadly equivalent to the English 'brick wall' against which the stubborn insist on knocking their heads. Yerma again invokes the proverbial power of water over stone ('a fuerza de caer la lluvia sobre las piedras éstas se ablandan') when she is discussing with María the efforts of her husband and two sisters-in-law to control her behaviour and the possible courses of action open to her. This time, though, she portrays herself figuratively as the opposing element, water: 'Son piedras delante de mí. Pero ellos no saben que yo, si quiero, puedo ser agua de arroyo que las lleve' (86). But for various reasons Yerma never really goes through with her threat, and the only instance of her overpowering strength comes at the very end, when she strangles Juan. Hence, in a last example of water imagery, one which involves a rare mention of the sea, Yerma is depicted as opposed to the water and also as recognizing its insuperable sway: '¡Está escrito y no me voy a poner a luchar a brazo partido con los mares!' (106).

The symbolism of the colour white works in a very different way. First of all, unlike water or dryness, the actual colour (*blanco, -a, blancura*, etc.) is only infrequently mentioned by name, and rather it is more usually brought to mind by a broad range of concrete beings and things that are typically or by definition white. Secondly, there are no real contrasts here: white is not played off against black or any other colour. Thirdly, whiteness has a very wide range of symbolic meanings, many of which are relevant here; indeed, whiteness can suggest so many things that on occasions two of them can themselves be in opposition. The symbolic polyvalency of whiteness lends itself, therefore, to the creation of complex, ambiguous meanings (*47*, p. 159). In the very first minutes of the action, we see Yerma trying to get Juan to drink a glass of milk in the hopes that it will build him up, because Juan looks pale and anaemic to her: 'ahora tienes la cara *blanca* como si no te diera en ella el sol' (32). This divergence, of whiteness as good, positive, life-giving, and simultaneously as bad, negative, life-threatening, runs through the whole play.

Sheep, lambs, flocks and wool are referred to with some frequency in the text, primarily because of Víctor's occupation and because keeping livestock is a major part of the activity of this agricultural community. The animals' most striking appearance is when the Lavanderas describe the departure of all the village flocks together:

LAVANDERA 1ª: ¿Se van ya los zagales?

LAVANDERA 3ª: Sí, ahora salen todos los rebaños.

LAVANDERA 4ª (*Respirando.*): Me gusta el olor de las ovejas.
[…]

LAVANDERA 5ª (*Mirando.*): Van juntos todos los rebaños.

LAVANDERA 4ª: Es una inundación de lana.
Arramblan con todo. Si los trigos verdes tuvieran cabeza, temblarían de verlos venir.

LAVANDERA 3ª: ¡Mira cómo corren! ¡Qué manada de enemigos! (69–70)

En masse they can be overwhelming and almost threatening, but nonetheless like white, foamy, free-flowing water (*50*, p. 50). Yerma offers a very different emotional tone when she imagines a husband taking good care of his ailing wife:

Mi mujer está enferma: voy a matar este cordero para hacerle un buen guiso de carne. […] voy a llevarle esta piel de oveja para guardar sus pies de la nieve. (33)

Notice here, as with 'vaso de leche' / 'cara blanca' (32), how 'piel de oveja' (good, warm) is immediately followed by 'nieve' (bad, cold). However, probably the most significant mention of these animals comes when Yerma is bewailing her lot, and sheep stand as the very embodiment of natural fertility: 'paren las ovejas cientos de corderos' (84).

Doves — white doves — are associated with Venus, and they are known for their billing and cooing. In the Lavanderas' scene, Lavandera 1ª sings of 'un niño pequeño, un niño' to which Lavandera 2ª replies: 'Y las palomas abren las alas y el pico' (73). Later doves are used as a metaphor for Yerma's breasts: '¡Ay, pechos ciegos bajo mi vestido! / ¡Ay, palomas sin ojos ni blancura!' (83). Just as the 'pechos' are 'ciegos' so the 'palomas' are now 'sin ojos', and the essential whiteness of the breasts is here negated — 'sin [...] blancura'.

Many materials and fabrics are also white: as bedsheets they are to be found on the nuptial bed and hence stand as an euphemistic image of sexual activity and the possibility of conception. Thus Yerma's reproaches, first in her memory of the wedding night: '¿No cantaba al levantar los embozos de holanda?' (34), and later in her complaint that nothing gets worn out by use in their house: 'Cuando [...] las sábanas de hilo se gastan con el uso' (78).[18] Identical associations are present in Víctor's song regarding the solitary rigours of a shepherd's life: '¿Por qué duermes solo, pastor? / En mi colcha de lana / dormirías mejor' (56), and in Lavandera 1ª's explicit assertion that: 'Hay que gemir en la sábana' (72).

Women's underclothes are usually white, and again there is a simple, straightforward logic to their connection with sexual activity and conception:

LAVANDERA 5ª: Dime si tu marido
guarda semilla
para que el agua cante

---

[18]'Embozo' is the turndown of a sheet; 'holanda' a finely woven material of cotton or linen, a luxury item suitable for this kind of special occasion.

por tu camisa.[19]

LAVANDERA 4ª: Es tu camisa
nave de plata y viento
por las orillas.

[…]

LAVANDERA 5ª: ¡Alegría, alegría, alegría
del vientre redondo bajo la camisa!
(71–73)

HEMBRA: Cuando llegue la noche de la romería
rasgaré los volantes de mi enagua.
(113)

MACHO: Si tú vienes a la romería
a pedir que tu vientre se abra,
no te pongas un velo de luto,
sino dulce camisa de holanda. (114)

Likewise, lace and linen can be used for making baby clothes: 'MARÍA: He comprado encajes, tres varas de hilo...' (37), 'MARÍA: Son los pañales' (43), 'YERMA: Corto unos pañales. […] Los voy a rodear de encajes' (44).

The light of dawn is white, and dawn, besides traditionally connoting a new start, renewed hope, rebirth, etc., is here repeatedly and explicitly associated with conception and childbirth:

LAVANDERA 5ª: Porque la luz se nos quiebra en la
garganta.

[…]

LAVANDERA 6ª (*Apareciendo en lo alto del
torrente.*):
Para que un niño funda
yertos vidrios del alba.

---

[19]The best translation here for 'camisa' would probably be chemise.

[…]

LAVANDERA 6ª: La aurora que mi niño
lleva en el delantal. (72–74)

YERMA: la rosa de maravilla.
Rayo de aurora parece (111)

MACHO: Vete sola detrás de los muros,
donde están las higueras cerradas,
y soporta mi cuerpo de tierra
hasta el blanco gemido del alba.
(114)

Yerma's longings for motherhood sometimes take concrete form in her imagining breast-feeding a baby, and of course both her skin and the milk are white. Thus:

¿Qué pides, niño, desde tan lejos? (*Pausa.*)
'Los blancos montes que hay en tu pecho.' (36)

Yo tengo la idea de que las recién paridas están como iluminadas por dentro, y los niños se duermen horas y horas sobre ellas oyendo ese arroyo de leche tibia que les va llenando los pechos para que ellos mamen, para que ellos jueguen, hasta que no quieran más, hasta que retiren la cabeza — 'otro poquito más, niño…' — , y se les llene la cara y el pecho de gotas blancas. (96–97)

Likewise, her frustration at her infertility sometimes manifests itself in a sense of the uselessness of her breasts:

Estos dos manantiales que yo tengo
de leche tibia, son en la espesura
de mi carne, dos pulsos de caballo,
que hacen latir la rama de mi angustia.
¡Ay, pechos ciegos bajo mi vestido!

¡Ay, palomas sin ojos ni blancura! (83–82)

The jasmine bush has a multitude of small white flowers, often likened to stars, and its characteristic perfume is strongest at night. In Yerma's poem or song she imagines her future child's reply to the most pressing of questions: '¿Cuándo, mi niño, vas a venir? (*Pausa.*) "Cuando tu carne huela a jazmín." ' (37, 45). The conjunction of 'carne' with 'jazmín' suggests a nocturnal erotic encounter, which will need to take place before Yerma can become pregnant. The oxymoronic or synaesthesic image of the 'jazmín caliente' appears three times in the Lavanderas' song (63, 70, 75). As a simile for 'la risa', the warmth of the smile is combined with the small, white jasmine-like teeth that would show as well as the sweet-smelling breath of the person, and as a poetic compliment that might be made by a man to a woman, it connotes happiness and physical attractiveness:

> Como un jazmín caliente
> tienes la risa.
> Quiero vivir
> en la nevada chica
> de ese jazmín. (70)

Whatever negative associations that the white snow might normally have are eliminated, rendered moot by the playful adjective 'nevada chica', and the passage in the song reads like a declaration of love or even a proposal of marriage. Lastly, the two Masks imagine the actions of the 'triste casada' in these terms:

> HEMBRA: ¡Ay, que el amor le pone
>   coronas y guirnaldas,
>
> [...]
>
> MACHO: Siete veces gemía,
>   nueve se levantaba;
>   quince veces juntaron
>   jazmines con naranjas. (114–15)

The whiteness and coolness of the jasmine flowers contrast with the warmth of the orange fruits, but in a transparent description of sexual intercourse, these elements or principles (abstinent, unfertilized, female / sexually active, fruitful, male) are brought together and joined in union ('juntaron'). Furthermore, there may also be a reminiscence of another white flower, the 'azahar' or orange blossom; brides in Andalusia were traditionally crowned with a garland of white orange blossoms, symbolizing their transition from a virginal, pre-marital state to the carnality and fecundity of marriage.

Frost and snow are mentioned on a few occasions; they are unequivocally negative, because they stand for coldness, but do not extend symbolically beyond that. Thus Yerma imagines a solicitous husband providing 'esta piel de oveja para guardar sus pies de la nieve' (33), and one aspect of the shepherd's hard life, roughing it in the countryside overnight, is expressed in a line of Víctor's song: 'y tu camisa de escarcha' (57).

The moon is one of the best known symbols in Lorca's poetic world, but in this play it is not to the forefront. In Víctor's quietistic acceptance of the world, it does not seem to be strongly characterized: 'La acequia por su sitio, el rebaño en el redil, la luna en el cielo y el hombre con su arado' (91). Elsewhere, however, it acquires a greater figurative charge: besides being white and nocturnal, the moon is a sterile, inert planet, which here may be its most important attribute. Thus in Yerma's description of a typical scene from the natural world:

> En el patio ladra el perro,
> en los árboles canta el viento.
> Los bueyes mugen al boyero
> y la luna me riza los cabellos. (36)

it would be much more logical for 'el aire' or 'el viento' to ruffle her hair; that the moon does so marks her out as especially 'touched' by the moon — and what it connotes. Likewise, in a similar conjunction

of elements, Yerma complains: 'que pido un hijo que sufrir y el aire /
me ofrece dalias de dormida luna!' (82).

This kind of absence, of lack, of blankness is the negative side
of *blancura*, and comes to symbolize Yerma's barrenness, infertility,
sterility. Thus Hombre 2° sings of the childless wife: '¡Ay, con el
vientre seco / y la color quebrada!' (113), and the Macho describes
her in the middle of the night, bathing in the river, as: '¡Ay, qué
blanca / la triste casada!' (114). Whiteness as connected with
cleanliness can also connote complete asepsia, the lack of life even at
the microbial level:

> LAVANDERA 4ª: Ella y las cuñadas, sin despegar los
> labios, blanquean todo el día las paredes, friegan los
> cobres, limpian con vaho los cristales, dan aceite a la
> solería. (68)

It is precisely this kind of sterile cleanliness and orderliness that
Yerma rejects: 'Cada noche, cuando me acuesto, encuentro mi cama
más nueva, más reluciente, como si estuviera recién traída de la
ciudad' (78).

Overall, then, the ambiguity and mix of values evidenced by
the symbolism of the colour white acts as a multi-faceted mirror of
Yerma's own situation. She is potentially fertile (white) but this is
never realized (white); rather she retains a kind of pure, almost
chaste quality (white) several years into her marriage (white), even
though she and her husband share the same bed (white). The flip side
of this condition is a kind of sterile blankness (white again) which
afflicts her life.

There is a fair amount of other imagery and symbolism
contained in the text, but nothing that approaches the magnitude and
significance of the two clusters just surveyed. The act of singing
acquires a considerable resonance here, associated not just with
joyfulness but specifically with sexual activity, pleasure and
conception (*6*, pp. 146–47; *22*, p. 173; *27*, p. 185). Yerma imagines
the scene when María first realized she was pregnant: 'Estarías
cantando, ¿verdad? Yo canto. ¿Tú?..., dime' (39), and the Vieja

describes her own experience of intercourse thus: 'Yo me he puesto boca arriba y he comenzado a cantar' (49). These early instances add significance to the scene between Víctor and Yerma, when the former is first heard singing off stage:

> YERMA: ¿Cantabas tú?
>
> VÍCTOR: Yo.
>
> YERMA: ¡Qué bien! Nunca te había sentido.
>
> VÍCTOR: ¿No?
>
> YERMA: Y qué voz tan pujante. Parece un chorro de agua que te llena toda la boca. (57–58)

Finally, the Lavanderas repeat the same ideas:

> LAVANDERA 1ª: Hay que gemir en la sábana.
>
> LAVANDERA 4ª: ¡Y hay que cantar! (72)
>
> LAVANDERA 1ª: Pero, ¡ay de la casada seca!
> [...]
>
> LAVANDERA 3ª: ¡Que cante!
>
> LAVANDERA 2ª: ¡Que se esconda!
>
> LAVANDERA 3ª: Y que vuelva a cantar. (74)

Flowers appear with some frequency (*22*, pp. 176–77). They are associated with sexual intercourse: 'LAVANDERA 3ª: Hay que juntar flor con flor / cuando el verano seca la sangre al segador' (72), 'MACHO: En esta romería / [...] las romeras [son] flores / para aquel que las gana' (115); with pregnancy: 'YERMA: te veo a ti y a las otras mujeres llenas por dentro de flores' (83); and, logically, when withered with old age: 'YERMA: Si pudiera de pronto volverme vieja y tuviera la boca como una flor machacada, te podría sonreír y conllevar la vida contigo' (79). Mentioned by name are hedge mustard, jasmine, rose, myrtle, wallflower, poppy and carnation. Unlike the imagery of water/dryness and whiteness, these do not derive so much from the surrounding physical environment but rather from the world of folklore and traditional song. I have already commented on Yerma's example of the 'jaramagos' (35) and the use of 'jazmín, jazmines'. In the Lavanderas' song where roses and wallflowers stand for male and female sexual organs (71-72), another verse mentions myrtle, a flower attributed to Venus, and when this is combined with the ardour of the husband, the sense is again transparent: 'LAVANDERA 5ª: Por el llano ya vino / mi marido a cenar. / Las brasas que me entrega / cubro con arrayán' (71). Carnations carry their usual connotations of romance and passion: 'YERMA: Cuando salía por mis claveles me tropecé con el muro' (104), and while 'la triste casada' is so white when she is bathing in the river, the Macho foresees her turning bright red with erotic fulfilment: 'Amapola y clavel serás luego, / cuando el macho despliegue su capa' (114). The rose, specifically 'la rosa amarilla' (that is, neither the white rose of purity nor the red rose of passion), is invoked a number of times in the prayer recited by the Mujeres as they make their way to the saint's chapel, the blossoming of the rose representing conception and pregnancy (110). Yerma develops this idea, imagining heaven as a kind of rose-garden and babies as heaven-sent:

> El cielo tiene jardines
> con rosales de alegría:
> entre rosal y rosal,
> la rosa de maravilla.
> [...]
> Señor, abre tu rosal
> sobre mi carne marchita. (110–111)

Furthermore, the rose can readily symbolize the mixture of beauty, joy and suffering that Yerma recognizes that children bring and which she willingly accepts: 'Abre tu rosa en mi carne / aunque tenga mil espinas' (111), ironically echoing Yerma's earlier admonition: 'Tener un hijo no es tener un ramo de rosas' (42).

The biblical symbol of the apple (from the Garden of Eden) appears a number of times, but with a variety of shifting connotations. Thus on the wedding night Yerma's exclamation, '¡Cómo huelen a manzana estas ropas!' (34), is sexually charged but full of positive promise for domestic happiness. As their relationship deteriorates, Lavandera 5ª asserts that a wife without children should properly be engaged in such homely (and decidedly non-sexual) activities as preparing 'confituras de manzanas' (65). At the beginning of Act II Juan complains:

> Ayer pasé un día duro. Estuve podando los manzanos y a la caída de la tarde me puse a pensar para qué pondría yo tanta ilusión en la faena si no puedo llevarme una manzana a la boca. (76)

In counterpoint to the domestic task of jam-making that Yerma never performs, Juan toils at the careful cultivation of apple trees for the economic rewards that this will bring. But literally and metaphorically, he cannot enjoy the fruit of his labours; he wears himself out in the orchards, his life with Yerma at home is filled with discord, and he can never engage in an act of pure and simple sexual pleasure with her — 'llevarme una manzana a la boca'. Juan's complaint is in a sense answered a little later, but not directly, for now Yerma is in conversation with Víctor: 'las mujeres somos otra cosa. Nunca oí decir a un hombre comiendo: "¡Qué buenas son estas manzanas!" Vais a lo vuestro sin reparar en las delicadezas' (89). While Juan grumbles about the lack of basic sexual gratification, Yerma counters that men are crude and unimaginative, going straight for sexual satisfaction without savouring the subtleties along the way.

The archetypal symbols of heat and cold take their place alongside those of wetness/dryness. In the specific similes and metaphors that appear here they generally need little explanation. Thus the Vieja: 'Tengo nueve hijos como nueve soles' (47); the

Hembra: 'La arena de las orillas / y el aire de la mañana / le daban fuego a su risa' (112); Lavandera 5ª: 'Las brasas que me entrega' (71); and Mujer 3ª: 'Y en el vientre de tus siervas, / la llama oscura de la tierra' (110). These brief images frame what is perhaps the most important single occurrence of the opposition, in Yerma's complaint about Juan:

> Cuando me cubre, cumple con su deber, pero yo le noto la cintura fría como si tuviera el cuerpo muerto, y yo, que siempre he tenido asco de las mujeres calientes, quisiera ser en aquel instante como una montaña de fuego. (98)

Furthermore, heat occasionally connotes the burning of longing: 'MUJER 2ª: Señor, calma con tu mano / las ascuas de su mejilla' (111). This line of verse casts a good deal of light on an otherwise rather mysterious detail, namely the faint burn mark that Yerma thinks she detects on Víctor's cheek (59): it is another token of their unspoken feelings.[20] Then again, heat in a very different context implies painful suffering: 'LAVANDERA 4ª: Cada hora que transcurre aumenta el infierno en aquella casa. [...] Pues, cuando más relumbra la vivienda, más arde por dentro' (68).

Finally, there is a miscellany of other instances of metaphorical language and symbolism dotted throughout the text; let us review a few representative examples. The bull's horn brandished by the Macho is of course a phallic symbol (112, 114, 115). The horse is a powerful, elegant animal, often associated with sexuality, and it is in this sense that we can understand the Vieja's comment to Yerma: '¿Quién puede decir que este cuerpo que tienes no es hermoso? Pisas y al fondo de la calle relincha el caballo' (49).[21] Later Yerma adapts the resounding of a horse's hoofbeats to render the pounding of her blood: 'Estos dos manantiales que yo tengo / de leche tibia, son en la espesura / de mi carne, dos pulsos de caballo'

---

[20]Francisco García Lorca explains how this symbol derives from an actual incident in Lorca's childhood (*23*, pp. 18–19).

[21]Cf. the white 'caballo garañón' in Act III of *La casa de Bernarda Alba*.

THE HENLEY COLLEGE LIBRARY

(82). A similar image returns a couple of pages later, where Yerma exclaims: 'mientras yo siento dos golpes de martillo aquí, en lugar de la boca de mi niño' (84). The hammer blows render the pain of her suffering while at the same time suggest pounding one's breast in futile rage.[22] More complex figurative expression is found in Yerma's lines: '¡Ay, qué dolor de sangre prisionera / me está clavando avispas en la nuca' (83). Established earlier is her conviction that 'cada mujer tiene sangre para cuatro o cinco hijos' (42–43), and so it becomes clear that 'sangre prisionera' is the unconceived, unborn child or children that Yerma believes herself to be physiologically capable of bearing. The acute pain of her frustration is rendered as wasp stings, but here again the language is heightened, with each sting likened in turn to a nail being driven into the nape of her neck, in a vision that is reminiscent of some of the more violent stories of Christian martyrdom. Unfortunately, and unbeknownst to her at the time, Yerma's choice of metaphor is all too accurate, as we shall see in chapter 8.

---

[22]Cf. the anvil image in 'Romance de la pena negra' (*Romancero gitano*).

6. Yerma's Predicament

Yerma longs to have a child, but does not. Why does she fix, so obsessively, her hopes and desires on this one event, why does she not conceive, and why does she not explore any of the other avenues open to her? These are some of the questions that this chapter will address. At the same time, from our perspective at the beginning of the twenty-first century, we must be careful to recognize, contextualize and historicize the gulf that separates us from Yerma's world and its *mores* and values. Social and scientific changes in the second half of the twentieth century, changes with which we are becoming increasingly familiar and comfortable, have radically altered our horizons and expectations. For instance, in Spain in the 1930s feminism was a small, marginal movement that only registered at all in the biggest cities — Madrid and Barcelona. Even more significantly, fertility drug treatments, artificial insemination, in vitro fertilization, surrogate motherhood and experiments with cloning, to say nothing of more basic concepts such as sperm motility or ovulation cycles, are now part of our everyday vocabulary, but they would have been as unimaginable and incomprehensible for the inhabitants of Yerma's village as, for example, the technology involved in landing a spacecraft on the moon.

Still, Yerma knows well enough that children result from sexual relations between men and women, even though explicit mention of the topic is for her associated with a sense of shame: 'No soy una casada indecente; pero yo sé que los hijos nacen del hombre y de la mujer' (98–99). Within Yerma's value system — which, as we have seen in chapter 3, she shares with the majority of the villagers — it is licit for such relations to occur only within the context of marriage; for Yerma, you have to be married to have children (*33*, p. 397), and she compliantly married the man that her father picked out for her. This is where it would appear that something has gone askew in Yerma's thinking and feelings. It is safe to assume that before her wedding she would have had no sexual experiences with a man and that her knowledge of sexual matters more broadly would have been sketchy and rudimentary; furthermore, as already noted, she likely did not know Juan all that well. Going into the marriage, then, would no doubt have been quite a frightening prospect, and yet at the same time we can imagine that it could also have inspired feelings of discovery, adventure, anticipation, or even excitement. Some of precisely these sentiments come through in María's description of her married life:

> YERMA: ¿Te quiere mucho?
>
> MARÍA: No me lo dice, pero se pone junto a mí y sus ojos tiemblan como dos hojas verdes.
>
> YERMA: ¿Sabía él que tú...?
>
> MARÍA: Sí.
>
> YERMA: ¿Y por qué lo sabía?
>
> MARÍA: No sé. Pero la noche que nos casamos me lo decía constantemente con su boca puesta en mi mejilla... (40–41)

But Yerma is not María. She knows of other young women who went to the nuptial bed gripped by fear and trepidation — 'Yo conozco muchachas que han temblado y que lloraron antes de entrar en la cama con sus maridos' (34) — and prides herself on the cheerfulness and purposefulness with which she approached the wedding night and the consummation of their marriage: '¿Lloré yo la primera vez que me acosté contigo? ¿No cantaba al levantar los embozos de holanda?' (34), 'Nadie se casó con más alegría' (34). Yet Yerma had no interest whatsoever in the sexual relations with her husband in and of themselves, but rather and solely as a means to an end, and that end is children. That is the only reason why she was happy on their wedding night. Sexual intercourse with Juan is therefore an activity to which Yerma submits, initially cheerfully and willingly, later increasingly grudgingly. It needs to be stressed that Yerma enters the marriage with this attitude towards her husband fully formed; it is not something that develops subsequently, for any of a variety of possible reasons, rather it is there from the very start (*40*, p. 69). As she confesses to the Vieja, she is not like some, perhaps most, other women, in that 'el primer día que me puse novia con él ya pensé... en los hijos' (50) — the thought was uppermost in her mind from the very first day of their engagement onwards. She skips right over the husband-wife relationship, romance, passion, sex, and any possible pleasure or fulfilment that these might bring her, to focus exclusively on the subsequent result. Thus inevitably sexual intercourse soon becomes an act of voluntary submission and a chore, though an essential one if she is to achieve her eventual goal: 'Yo me entregué a mi marido por él [mi hijo], y me sigo entregando para ver si llega, pero nunca por divertirme' (51; *37*, p. 291).

This last is a crucial comment — 'pero nunca por divertirme'. It is only possible to speculate on the reasons for Yerma's absolute ruling out of the expectation or receipt of any physical satisfaction, but whatever the cause her position is extreme (*6*, pp. 150–51). Is it perhaps her overdeveloped sense of shame that inhibits her, as a result of an excessively strict and austere upbringing in her parents' house? (*27*, p. 184; *3*, p. 19). Has she misinterpreted or been misled as to doctrinal Catholic teaching on the issue? (*8*, pp. 53, 59 n14; *19*, pp. 203, 205; *33*, p. 397; *38*, p. 75). As we saw in chapter 3, the orthodox line is that sexual relations within marriage are primarily for the purposes of procreation and only very secondarily for the relief of concupiscence, but where the church teaches 'primarily', has Yerma substituted 'solely'? Martín points out that there is a strong tradition in Spain of a double standard, of permitting concupiscence in the husband but of de-sexualizing the wife and making her ideal the Virgin Mary, the non-sexual mother *par excellence* (*33*, pp. 400–10; *35*, pp. 237–38). Both possible explanations for her behaviour are evinced in one of her later remarks:

> Cuando me cubre, cumple con su deber, pero yo le noto
> la cintura fría como si tuviera el cuerpo muerto, y yo,
> que siempre he tenido asco de las mujeres calientes,
> quisiera ser en aquel instante como una montaña de
> fuego. (98)

Here she sees their relations as a duty that Juan periodically performs
as part of his church-sanctioned marital responsibilities, while the
revulsion that she says she feels seems to be more related to shame
or even a personal distaste for sex (or sexual arousal) under any
guise.

This in turn is connected in Yerma's mind not only with the
nature of and motivation for sexual relations between husband and
wife, but also with the whole issue of human relations between man
and woman. As she asks rhetorically in conversation with the Vieja:

> ¿Es preciso buscar en el hombre al hombre nada más?
> Entonces, ¿qué vas a pensar cuando te deja en la cama
> con los ojos tristes mirando al techo y da media vuelta y
> se duerme? ¿He de quedarme pensando en él o en lo que
> puede salir relumbrando de mi pecho? (51)

Yerma's comments do not say much for Juan as a lover, which may
be a further, contributory part of her problem (7, p. 463), but at the
same time she seems to be generalizing far beyond her individual
experiences with her own husband. Indeed, she appears to perceive
both broadly human and specifically sexual relations within marriage
as unsatisfactory, disappointing, incomplete, and transitory, whereas
what she desires is clearly more personal and more transcendent. The
verb 'buscar' is highly significant here, as it will reappear later in the
play on three separate occasions (37, p. 286). In Yerma's last,
desperate but doomed attempt at a reconciliation with Juan she is
perhaps trying to convince herself as much as her husband:

> YERMA (*En un arranque y abrazándose a su marido.*):
> Te busco a ti. Te busco a ti. Es a ti a quien busco día y

noche sin encontrar sombra donde respirar. Es tu sangre
y tu amparo lo que deseo.

JUAN: ¡Apártate! (103)

Here Yerma appears to be heeding (momentarily) the advice of other
villagers in her reference to a model of marital and male-female
relations which many of them promote: 'VIEJA: Son los hombres los
que te tienen que amparar' (52), 'VIEJA 1ª: ...debes ampararte en el
amor de tu marido' (98). However, it is a bitter irony that,
figuratively speaking, she has to search for Juan in Dolores's house
and not their own (*12*, p. 26). Furthermore, her stated desire for 'tu
sangre' (in effect, his semen) alongside 'tu amparo' shows that she
can never renounce or forget her primary goal of prolonging the
bloodline. With no help or encouragement coming from Juan's
brusque and cold rebuff, she cannot maintain for very long any
appreciation of the potential compensations or solace of the kind of
arrangement implied by 'amparo', and she fails to shake off her
deep-seated conviction as to its flaws and shortcomings. This is clear
both in her out-of-hand rejection of the Vieja's offer to go and live
with her and one of her sons: 'Yo no puedo ir a buscar' (118), and
shortly thereafter in the annoyance and disgust she expresses during
her and Juan's final confrontation: 'Me buscas como cuando te
quieres comer una paloma' (123; see chapter 8).

As a consequence, then, of her dissatisfaction with the
limitations, in her opinion, of husband-wife relations, and her general
disapproval or distaste for the whole erotic facet of marriage, Yerma
exclusively invests the goals of conception, pregnancy, childbirth,
and motherhood with the ability to provide her with fulfilment (*32*,
p. 20). This attitude links up with several aspects of the value-system
of the community where she lives (see chapter 3), with the result that
for Yerma — as, one suspects, for many in her position — both
one's self-worth and one's sense of femininity are rooted in
achieving the objective of childbearing and motherhood: 'JUAN: No
maldigas. Está feo en una mujer. YERMA: Ojalá fuera yo una
mujer' (62). She has bought into the system, she has conformed, she
has done what society expects of her, she has had sexual intercourse

with her husband, and she has waited, and yet she has not conceived; hence, there is a tremendous irony for her in that without children she is still considered a married woman and is still required to comply with all the other obligations that that station brings with it: '(*Con asombro.*): ¡Casada!' (81; *54*, p. 129).

Yerma's fixation on motherhood makes her something of an expert on the subject, even if her knowledge is based on observation rather than first-hand experience. Thus she is full of good practical advice for María, who has just become pregnant. Remarking that 'siempre oí decir que las primerizas tienen susto' (43), Yerma counsels her: 'No andes mucho y, cuando respires, respira tan suave como si tuvieras una rosa entre los dientes' (40); 'No corras por las piedras de la calle' (43). María also refers to feeling the baby kicking: 'MARÍA: Oye, dicen que más adelante te empuja suavemente con las piernecitas. YERMA: Y entonces es cuando se le quiere más, cuando se dice ya ¡mi hijo!' (40). Yerma's own view of motherhood is a mixture of pragmatism and idealism, of a willing acceptance of the many pains and tribulations and an eager anticipation of the joyful, tender moments. We can see the former attitude when she is swopping stories with María:

MARÍA: [El niño] Lloraba como un torito, con la fuerza de mil cigarras cantando a la vez, y nos orinaba y nos tiraba de las trenzas y, cuando tuvo cuatro meses, nos llenaba la cara de arañazos.

YERMA (*Riendo.*): Pero esas cosas no duelen.

MARÍA: Te diré...

YERMA: ¡Bah! Yo he visto a mi hermana dar de mamar a su niño con el pecho lleno de grietas y le producía un gran dolor, pero era un dolor fresco, bueno, necesario para la salud.

MARÍA: Dicen que con los hijos se sufre mucho.

YERMA: Mentira. Eso lo dicen las madres débiles, las quejumbrosas. ¿Para qué los tienen? Tener un hijo no es

> tener un ramo de rosas. Hemos de sufrir para verlos
> crecer. Yo pienso que se nos va la mitad de nuestra
> sangre. Pero esto es bueno, sano, hermoso. Cada mujer
> tiene sangre para cuatro o cinco hijos... (42–43)

She is also highly, some would say over-, protective: 'Sí, pero es que no os dais cuenta de lo que es un niño pequeño. La causa que nos parece más inofensiva puede acabar con él. Una agujita, un sorbo de agua' (53–54). Muchacha 2ª believes that Yerma would not be that way if she actually had four or five of her own to contend with, but Yerma rejects any such thoughts out of hand: 'Aunque tuviera cuarenta' (54). Counterbalancing her recognition of suffering and tribulations, the simple but profound fulfilment that Yerma also imagines and aspires to comes through clearly in her dialogue with Dolores:

> A mí no me da asco de mi hijo. Yo tengo la idea de que
> las recién paridas están como iluminadas por dentro, y
> los niños se duermen horas y horas sobre ellas oyendo
> ese arroyo de leche tibia que les va llenando los pechos
> para que ellos mamen, para que ellos jueguen, hasta que
> no quieran más, hasta que retiren la cabeza — 'otro
> poquito más, niño...' — , y se les llene la cara y el pecho
> de gotas blancas. (96–97)

As for childlessness, Yerma claims that it is impossible for women who have experienced motherhood to comprehend what an infertile woman goes through: 'Las mujeres, cuando tenéis hijos, no podéis pensar en las que no los tenemos. Os quedáis frescas, ignorantes, como el que nada en agua dulce no tiene idea de la sed' (84–85). She also asserts her own desire for a clearer understanding of her condition: 'Hace tiempo estoy deseando tener conversación con mujer vieja. Porque yo quiero enterarme' (48); she complains about the shroud of mystery that surrounds the whole topic of conception and pregnancy: 'todas estas cosas dicen que no se pueden saber' (51); and she laments that wiser or more satisfactory explanations of life's enigmas are closed off from her: '¡Qué pena más grande no poder sentir las enseñanzas de los viejos!' (91; *51*, p. 119).[23] But above all, throughout the play, in conversation with many of the other characters and in moments of poetic soliloquy (36–37, 82–83), she gives repeated voice to her own longing for motherhood and the suffering that she experiences as a result of her childlessness.

A sampling of these exchanges will illustrate Yerma's growing frustration over the course of the years:

> YERMA: No tenemos hijos… ¡Juan!
> […]
>
> YERMA: No. No me repitas lo que dicen. Yo veo por mis ojos que eso no puede ser. (34–35)

> VÍCTOR: Bueno, pues a ver si con el ejemplo te animas. En esta casa hace falta un niño.
>
> YERMA (*Con angustia.*): ¡Hace falta! (45)

> VIEJA: ¿Tienes hijos?
>
> YERMA: No.
>
> VIEJA: ¡Bah! ¡Ya tendrás!
>
> YERMA (*Con ansia.*): ¿Usted lo cree?
>
> VIEJA: ¿Por qué no? (47)

> JUAN: ¿Es que te falta algo? Dime. (*Pausa.*) ¡Contesta!

---

[23]It is hard to know exactly what Yerma means by both 'las enseñanzas' and 'los viejos' here, but she seems to be referring to olden times rather than just the older generation. The phrase is highly reminiscent of the more explicit comment made by Bernarda in *La casa de Bernarda Alba* to the effect that 'Los antiguos sabían muchas cosas que hemos olvidado'.

YERMA (*Con intención y mirando fijamente al
marido.*): Sí, me falta. (79)

YERMA (*A gritos.*): Maldito sea mi padre, que me dejó
su sangre de padre de cien hijos. Maldita sea mi sangre,
que los busca golpeando por las paredes. (104)

Furthermore, she declares that she is prepared to resort to extreme
measures, if necessary, in order to bring about the desired outcome
of childbearing, and through her figurative language we get a sense
of both her desolation and her stern resolve: 'Usted me ha de decir lo
que tengo que hacer, que yo haré lo que sea, aunque me mande
clavarme agujas en el sitio más débil de mis ojos' (49). Indeed, such
is the intensity of her longing to have a child of her own that we tend
to believe her when she asserts that 'aunque yo supiera que mi hijo
me iba a martirizar después y me iba a odiar y me iba a llevar de los
cabellos por las calles, recibiría con gozo su nacimiento…' (97–98).

Later, she puts this determination into practice by engaging the
assistance of Dolores 'la conjuradora', who offers as a remedy a
typically folkloric mix of superstition, herbal potions, white magic
and elements of Christianity.[24] After the spells and prayers have
been recited in the cemetery in the middle of the night, Dolores
comments on Yerma's outstanding courage (95), to which Yerma
laconically replies: 'Yo he venido por el resultado' (96). However,
despite Dolores's protestations of trustworthiness and truthfulness
(one assumes that some payment for her services was involved), the
whole account that she gives of the last woman whom she helped,
who supposedly went into labour, with twins no less, only moments
after the last prayers were said (96), comes across as highly
exaggerated and utterly implausible. But Yerma, through her naiveté,
or perhaps her pressing psychological need to believe, nonetheless
appears to accept this 'old wives' tale' at face value (96–97). The
further irony, of course, is that the Muchacha 2ª, Dolores's daughter

---

[24]Cf. the chapter on the supernatural in Pitt-Rivers's *The People of the
Sierra*.

who arranged the meeting, herself remains childless, despite her own mother's best efforts to bring about her pregnancy (54; *1*, p. 30; *11*, p. 81).

Although, as has already been established, none of the villagers could possibly have any knowledge or understanding of the actual medical factors involved here (*48*, p. 19), this does not stop several of them — as well as Yerma herself — from attributing responsibility or blame for her condition, which may be termed childlessness, infertility or barrenness/sterility depending on the point of view adopted. As we have seen, Lavandera 1ª believes that Yerma is not to blame (65) and rather that Juan is at fault (68); she is immediately contradicted by Lavandera 4ª, who squarely lays the problem at Yerma's feet (68). In Act I, Scene ii, the Vieja strongly insinuates that it is Juan who is to blame, without going so far as to state this outright, and Yerma does not fully comprehend what she is saying (52). But by Act III, Scene ii, the Vieja no longer feels the need for discretion or restraint:

> VIEJA: Antes no he podido decirte nada, pero ahora sí.
>
> YERMA: ¡Y qué me vas a decir que ya no sepa!
>
> VIEJA: Lo que ya no se puede callar. Lo que está puesto encima del tejado. La culpa es de tu marido. ¿Lo oyes? Me dejaría cortar las manos. (117)

Early on, Yerma is indignant at what she perceives as the unfairness, the unjustness of the situation (41, 48), and wonders aloud whether '¿tengo yo la culpa?' (51), and if so, why that should be so (*48*, p. 25). But towards the end of the play, Juan's attitude of steadfast indifference to their continuing childless state and his growing irritation with her 'obsession' lead her to propose her own explanation: 'Lo que pasa es que él [Juan] no ansía hijos. […] Se lo conozco en la mirada y, como no los ansía, no me los da' (99). When Juan confronts her in Dolores's house, Yerma counters his accusations with a laconic and cryptic response that may well carry the innuendo of his responsibility: 'Yo no sé por qué empiezan los

malos aires que revuelcan al trigo y ¡mira tú si el trigo es bueno!'
(103).[25] However, the last time the word 'culpa' is actually uttered
on stage, it is, significantly, in the mouth of Juan, who states simply
and emphatically that 'No tenemos culpa ninguna' (121).

This is surely the crux of the matter. While different characters
have their different opinions as to cause or fault, Yerma's childlessness is just how things are, and nobody is to blame, or at least it is
impossible to pin the blame on any single individual (*14*, p. 88; *20*,
p. 22; *34*, p. 234; *47*, p. 157).[26] While there are occasional red
herrings like the Vieja's allusion to 'simiente podrida' (chapter 2),
the play is not ultimately about physiology or biology. After all, the
action is set in rural Spain in the 1930s or possibly earlier, and to
engage in idle — and anachronistic — speculation about Juan's low
sperm count or Yerma's blocked fallopian tubes is simply to miss the
point. To try to identify either Yerma or Juan as the culprit is to enter
into a kind of guessing game that the text of the play deliberately
ensures has no solution, no answer.[27] The reasons (if they can be
called reasons) for Yerma's childlessness will be explored later in
this chapter and the next, but before proceeding we need to look for a
moment at the possible remedies and alternatives available to Yerma
to bring about an end to her unwanted infertile condition.

---

[25]This barbed comment can be read in at least two ways: Yerma is the 'good
wheat' which is potentially fruitful and bountiful, while Juan is cast as the
'malos aires' that beat down the wheat and thereby negate its potential
qualities. Or again, Yerma is the wheat which is inherently good, 'los malos
aires' are the foundless rumours that circulate and damage her reputation just
as they would damage the wheat (*8*, p. 48).

[26]In an analysis of early criticism, Allen crushingly demonstrates how futile
is speculation about Yerma's or Juan's degree of responsibility and about
their possible physiological affliction (female infertility, frigidity, male
sterility, impotence, etc.) (*6*, pp. 125–32).

[27]This undecidability is reflected in Yerma's name: one dictionary (María
Moliner) gives as a definition of the noun 'yermo' 'terreno [...] no
cultivable o no cultivado'. Compare too Lorca's trenchant interview
statement: 'Nada de análisis, que es lo que más fácilmente hubiera logrado
con mi disposición psicológica para ahondar de un modo tremendo en las
causas' (197).

First of all, we know that Yerma, with a kind of grim determination, carries on having sexual relations with Juan right up to near the end of the play, despite the fact that she is increasingly reluctant and it is increasingly unpleasant for her to participate. She knows that this is still the best — really the only — way to try and bring about a pregnancy, however unlikely that seems as the years pass and nothing happens. Thus in Act I, Scene ii, Yerma tells the Vieja that 'me sigo entregando para ver si llega' (51); by Act III, Scene i, she comments that 'cuando me cubre, cumple con su deber' (98) and 'no lo quiero, no lo quiero y, sin embargo, es mi única salvación' (99) — salvation in the sense that he is the only person, as her sexual partner, who can give her a child. Later in the same scene she takes the initiative and even attempts, momentarily, to patch things up with Juan (103-04). Indeed, it is suggested on more than one occasion through the play that if Yerma could only bring herself to respond to Juan sexually and passionately, then she would conceive, but of course this never happens (*6*, p. 145; *7*, p. 462; *48*, p. 25). The Vieja's perspective is that 'los hombres tiene que gustar, muchacha' (50), and as someone who has given birth fourteen times (48), she is invested with more than a certain authority. Ironically, Yerma seems to know as much herself, but it never becomes more than an unconscious intuition. Speaking precisely of her infertility, to María she confides that 'muchas veces salgo descalza al patio para pisar la tierra, no sé por qué' (41), an action that acquires its full definition only when we discover that the masks of Macho and Hembra have 'un sentido de pura tierra' (112). Likewise, she unknowingly supplies her own answer in the verse dialogue with her longed-for child: '¿Cuando, mi niño, vas a venir? (*Pausa.*) / "Cuando tu carne huela a jazmín"' (37); her flesh smelling of the sweetly-scented, nocturnal flower clearly connotes a passionate physical encounter which, as the subjunctive form of the verb ('huela') anticipates, never comes to be (*39*, p. 22).

Beyond this basic strategy of continued sexual relations, Yerma also has recourse to Dolores 'la conjuradora' and her folk spells and prayers, and she attends the *romería* at the shrine of the saint who is supposed to help barren women. Apart from this, there is little left for Yerma to do but wait and hope, for all other potential remedies are deemed untenable (*8*, p. 54). Divorce in this traditional, Catholic country, is of course not even a possibility, and is never even mentioned.[28] Leaving Juan permanently for another man, or committing adultery within their marriage, are equally repugnant options to Yerma (*1*, p. 22; *27*, p. 159). The Vieja provides the opportunity for the former at the *romería*:

> Mi hijo está sentado detrás de la ermita esperándome. Mi
> casa necesita una mujer. Vete con él y viviremos los tres
> juntos. Mi hijo sí es de sangre. Como yo. Si entras en mi
> casa, todavía queda olor de cunas. (118)

but it is an offer that Yerma rejects out of hand. The opportunity for the latter would seem to be presented in the character of Víctor, about whom the Lavanderas gossip and for whom Yerma feels something special, but as we have seen in their encounters during the play, neither acts on any feelings they may have (cf. chapter 2). Finally, Juan suggests that Yerma bring into their house a child that she could mother, but again Yerma immediately rules this out:

> JUAN: ¿Por qué no te traes un hijo de tu hermano? Yo
> no me opongo.

> YERMA: No quiero cuidar hijos de otras. Me figuro que
> se me van a helar los brazos de tenerlos. (80)

So, to return to two of our opening questions, why does Yerma want a child so desperately, and since she does, why are these various alternative avenues so unthinkable for her? Clearly, part of the answer to the first is that Yerma has internalized most of the social attitudes and values of her environment (*24*, p. 250; *54*, p. 128; see chapter 3), but there are psychological issues at work here too

---

[28]In fact, a law establishing civil divorce (under limited circumstances) was passed by the Republican government in early 1932, but again this has nothing to do with the kind of world that Yerma lives in.

(*27*, p. 184). Her sense of shame, the strict style of her upbringing, combining with social ideas of decency and traditional religious teaching, all lead her to be uninterested in sex for its own sake and to shift her focus exclusively to childbearing. Furthermore, in psychological terms, motherhood seems to her satisfying on a personal basis and a validation of her own femininity; in social terms, motherhood is validating within the community, for this is what women are supposed to do (*37*, p. 286; *48*, p. 24; *49*, p. 274). Maternity, then, would give her a reason for her life and a reason to live.

Psychological and social factors also combine to eliminate any other course of action for Yerma than to stay with Juan and keep on trying to have a child. She is very much her own person, she has a strong sense of identity, and to go elsewhere in search of children seems to her like a betrayal of her very selfhood: 'Yo no puedo ir a buscar' (118; *15*, p. 126). Society dictates that childbearing must occur within marriage, and infidelity or abandonment are strongly discouraged by gossip and social opprobrium. If Yerma chafes at some of the restrictions, she never goes beyond the boundaries, and while the Vieja urges her 'no te importe la gente' (118), clearly they do. In addition, Yerma has a strongly developed sense of honour and of family, and honour too sets norms of conduct that bind her to her husband and prevent her from behaving in any kind of radically unorthodox fashion — as she puts it 'El agua no se puede volver atrás, ni la luna llena sale al mediodía' (118; *1*, pp. 21–22). Lorca was fully cognizant of the severity of these limitations: 'Mi protagonista tiene limitado su arbitrio, encadenada por el concepto, que va disuelto en su sangre, de la honra españolísima' (197). Yerma's predicament, then, has no solution, no way out (*14*, p. 89).

Beyond this spread of psychological and social considerations, there are still further motives why Yerma wants a child so badly. Living as she does in an agricultural community, where crops are grown and animals are bred, she longs to be an active, contributing part of nature, to participate fully in that natural cycle of conception, birth and upbringing (*14*, p. 87; *15*, p. 125; *37*, p. 289; *49*, p. 267; *52*,

p. 175). That she does not, that she cannot, is both an offence to her and demeaning or humiliating:

> Que estoy ofendida, ofendida y rebajada hasta lo último, viendo que los trigos apuntan, que las fuentes no cesan de dar agua, y que paren las ovejas cientos de corderos, y las perras, y que parece que todo el campo puesto de pie me enseña sus crías tiernas, adormiladas, mientras yo siento dos golpes de martillo aquí, en lugar de la boca de mi niño. (84)

Lorca commented in an interview precisely on this sense of disjunction that Yerma experiences:

> *Yerma* [...] es, sobre todas las cosas, la imagen de la fecundidad castigada a la esterilidad. [...] Yo he querido hacer, he hecho, a través de la línea muerta de lo infecundo, el poema vivo de la fecundidad. Y es de ahí, del contraste de lo estéril y lo vivificante, de donde extraigo el perfil trágico de la obra. (160)

In addition, as already seen, Yerma finds no satisfaction in the act of sexual intercourse itself, but through her insertion in the natural cycle, through the ability to conceive and hence create, she believes she would indeed attain a kind of fulfilment: '¿He de quedarme pensando en él [el hombre] o en lo que puede salir relumbrando de mi pecho?' (51).[29] But there is a false dichotomy here in Yerma's thinking or feelings, for it could well be argued that it is precisely Nature (that she so wants to be a part of) that has favoured the preservation and multiplication of the human species by ensuring that coition is an act that is usually so pleasurable and physically gratifying (6, pp. 153–54). Consequently, instead of finding satis-

---

[29]'Pecho', associated metonymically with the heart, and lexically with breasts and breast-feeding, also therefore alludes to the womb from which her child would actually emerge.

faction in the present, Yerma looks beyond the mechanics of creation itself into the future, anticipating a kind of continuity in which her child — here specified as her son — would carry on from her and achieve (unspecified) goals that she has already established: 'Yo pienso muchas cosas, muchas, y estoy segura que las cosas que pienso las ha de realizar mi hijo' (51; *41*, pp. 65–66).

Yerma therefore experiences her childlessness as a dryness, a void, an absence, a lack, and a kind of impoverishment: 'YERMA (*Con angustia.*): ¡Hace falta [un niño]!' (45), 'YERMA: ¿Por qué estoy yo seca?' (48), 'VIEJA: ¡Y resulta que estás vacía!' (51), 'YERMA (*Con intención y mirando fijamente al marido.*): Sí, me falta' (79), 'YERMA: No es envidia lo que tengo; es pobreza' (83). A multitude of circumstances have conspired to leave her wanting a child, childless, and with no means to bring an end to her childlessness. Her most basic desire — effectively, her only desire — is unfulfilled and denied, and so her frustration is all-encompassing.

But this brings us back to Yerma and her name. Within the context of the action, Yerma is born to be barren and hence frustrated, because within the context of the script of the play, she has been named Yerma (*1*, p. 27; *14*, p. 89; *18*, p. 11; *37*, p. 285; *47*, p. 157). Here, the experience of the text will be very different for reader and spectator. The reader relentlessly sees Yerma's name preceding each speech, each piece of dialogue, but what the audience-member hears is very different. Beyond the title of the play, *Yerma*, printed on billboards and in programmes, Yerma's name is not heard on stage until the very end of Act II, Scene ii, after Víctor has left and after Yerma has crept away to Dolores's house (*6*, p. 155; *22*, p. 171). The Cuñadas call out her name three times in a growing crescendo, an act made all the more noticeable and significant by their own spinsterly condition and the fact that they have not uttered a single word on stage up to this point :

CUÑADA 1ª (*En voz baja.*): ¡Yerma!

(*Sale la* HERMANA 2ª, *se miran las dos y se dirigen a la puerta.*)

CUÑADA 2ª (*Más alto.*): ¡Yerma! (*Sale.*)

CUÑADA 1ª (*Dirigiéndose a la puerta también y con
una imperiosa voz.*): ¡Yerma! (94)

Her name has finally been spoken aloud and, in terms of the action,
it could be argued that it is at this moment, as Act II ends, that her
fate is sealed, with Víctor's definitive removal from the field of
possibility while the mournful shepherds' horns echo in the distance
(*8*, p. 54).[30] But from another perspective, she is really defined from
the outset, from baptism (by Enrique her father or by Lorca her
author), frustration will be her essential condition, and there is
nothing to be done, even though, within the action, neither she nor
any of the other characters ever actually comments on her outlandish
name or appears to realize what it means for her — it is as if it were
transparent to them. Everything, then, is determined from the start:
although Yerma does not know it, because she is called Yerma she
cannot, by definition, hope to have children, even though, as it
happens, that is the one thing she does want to do. The range of
implications of this at-first-sight strange and disconcerting situation
will be the subject of the next chapter.

---

[30]Yerma is addressed only once more by name in the rest of the play, by
Dolores in Act III, Scene i, who rebukes her with the exclamation '¡Yerma!'
(98) — a further irony, given what the 'conjugadora' is supposed to be doing
for her (*3*, p. 28).

7. Yerma's Struggle

Some critics have found *Yerma* rather lacking in dramatic terms because of the relative paucity of plot development (*22*, p. 166; *53*, p. 198), and it is undeniably true that little happens and there are no real twists or turns in the story until the shocking denouement. On the other hand, this was an effect that Lorca, as we have seen (chapter 4), was perfectly conscious of having created, and one must presume that he had his reasons. I believe that part of the explanation is the fact that the literal level of the action already comes very close to the more abstract level of the theme, without the need for further elaboration; the presentation of Yerma's barely changing predicament serves, in and of itself, to provide almost all the necessary material for the interpretative leap that seeks to tease out the broader implications of the play.

A resident of this farming community and surrounded by the countryside, every day Yerma encounters concrete examples and reminders of the natural cycle of birth, life and death that governs the existence of all living things, plants, animals and human beings (chapter 5). In the light of this, we can read Yerma's longing for childbearing and motherhood in two different, though comple-mentary, ways. In one sense her basic desire is reasonable and realistic, in that she merely wants to participate fully in that natural cycle and not be excluded from it. In a second sense, though, her longings go much further and are much more ambitious, in that procreation is the only way for her to break the cycle or at least not be completely controlled by it; while she as an individual will inevitably be subject to the natural laws of aging and mortality, part of her would live on in the child or children she would give birth to (*15*, pp. 126–27, 129).

Now, most (though not all) human beings can have a child if they want to, but no one can achieve individual immortality. On a thematic level, then, *Yerma* is about the frustration or negation of that very human desire for transcendence, of that longing for immortality, to cheat death. On a literal level, this is presented within a specific set of circumstances as the frustration/negation of what is a much more modest and attainable aspiration, namely childbearing, but where childbearing carries with it, both inherently and figuratively, immediate connotations of the perpetuation of the self and a partial victory over individual mortality (*16*; *53*, pp. 195–96). This last notion is a fundamental and age-old philosophical proposition that is already to be found, for instance, in Plato's writings: in the *Symposium*, Diotima argues that 'there is something divine in this process; this is how mortal creatures achieve immortality, in pregnancy and giving birth. [...] reproduction is the closest mortals can come to being permanently alive and immortal' (*53*, pp. 197–98).[31] Yerma is Yerma and is named Yerma because, as the protagonist of the play, she is called upon to experience and live out the frustration of the desire for transcendence/immortality as the frustration of her desire for children.

This can be observed in the attitudes that Yerma adopts in the course of the play, in the vocabulary that she uses to lament her condition, and in the way in which both attitudes and vocabulary immediately lead us to much wider issues. First of all, her situation seems to her entirely unfair, unjust and undeserved, since, as far as can be determined, she is not at fault and most probably no one is (see the section on 'blame' in chapter 6). Thus Yerma repeatedly complains about her lot, questioning the apparent arbitrariness with which she has been singled out for the affliction of barrenness: 'Pienso que no es justo que yo me consuma aquí' (41); '¿Por qué estoy yo seca? ¿Me he de quedar en plena vida para cuidar aves o poner cortinitas planchadas en mi ventanillo? No' (48); 'Roca que es una infamia que sea roca, porque debía ser un canasto de flores y agua dulce' (80); '¡Cómo no me voy a quejar cuando te veo a ti y a

---

[31]Plato, *The Symposium*, trans. Christopher Gill (Harmondsworth: Penguin, 1999), pp. 43–44 (Stephanus 206c–207a).

las otras mujeres llenas por dentro de flores, y viéndome yo inútil en medio de tanta hermosura!' (83).

Next, what most obviously articulates the succession of the three acts of the play is the passage of time (chapter 4). Yerma's situation remains unchanged in that she continues childless, but it does change in other respects, in that all the while she is acutely conscious of the years passing and of the receding likelihood of her ever conceiving (*2*, p. 25; *6*, p. 132; *23*, p. 348). Yerma loses out on both counts, and she expresses the pain and unfairness of this in graphically concrete terms:

> Justo. Las mujeres dentro de sus casas. Cuando las casas
> no son tumbas. Cuando las sillas se rompen y las sábanas
> de hilo se gastan con el uso. Pero aquí, no. Cada noche,
> cuando me acuesto, encuentro mi cama más nueva, más
> reluciente, como si estuviera recién traída de la ciudad.
> (78)

She experiences a kind of 'living death' ('casas […] tumbas'), for it is as if she were suspended (death) in time (life). She would be willing to accept the trade-off of being subject to the laws of nature (and, one might add, society) if only they would operate fully within her household, that is, she would welcome the signs of mutability and wear and tear because they would also be tokens of dynamic, purposeful activity including, needless to say, the bringing-up of children. As it is, the environment inside her house remains sterile and aseptic, reflecting her infertility (chapter 5; *38*, p. 76).

Two statements that Yerma makes later in the play add to and further elucidate our understanding of this point. To the Vieja 1ª's practical question: 'Pero, ¿qué vega esperas dar a tu hijo, ni qué felicidad, ni qué silla de plata?' she replies dismissively: 'Yo no pienso en el mañana; pienso en el hoy. Tú estás vieja y lo ves ya todo como un libro leído' (97).[32] To Juan she tries to explain the root of

---

[32]There are several layers of reference and meaning in the Vieja's phrase 'silla de plata'. In the poem 'Cancioncilla sevillana' from Lorca's collection

her suffering: 'Si pudiera de pronto volverme vieja y tuviera la boca como una flor machacada, te podría sonreír y conllevar la vida contigo' (79). That is to say, it is because she is still young that this situation is so galling; she is in the prime of her child-bearing years, yet nothing is happening, and she has decades to live through before the approach of old age and the relief that this might bring (see chapter 9).

Yerma's attitudes towards time and aging serve to explain why she is so wounded by what the Vieja says to her towards the end of Act III, Scene ii. The Vieja, her offer spurned, lets loose some spiteful, retaliatory remarks before going off to rejoin her son:

> VIEJA (*Fuerte.*): Pues sigue así. Por tu gusto es. Como los cardos del secano, pinchosa, marchita.

> YERMA (*Fuerte.*): Marchita sí, ¡ya lo sé! ¡Marchita! No es preciso que me lo refriegues por la boca. No vengas a solazarte como los niños pequeños en la agonía de un animalito. Desde que me casé estoy dándole vueltas a esta palabra, pero es la primera vez que la oigo, la primera vez que me la dicen en la cara. La primera vez que veo que es verdad. (119)

The importance and impact of the adjective have to do, I believe, with the process that it implies. The selfsame Vieja, in Act I, Scene ii, had described Yerma as '¡ay, qué flor abierta!' (51). Now, here, the word *marchito, -a* as applied precisely to flowers, denotes those that have shrivelled up and withered. It is as if the bloom of her youth were over, the flower of her prime gone before its time. We need to remember that although five years have elapsed since their wedding, Yerma is still a young woman, but in facing up to the truth

---

Canciones, one of the stanzas reads as follows: '(Sillita de oro / para el moro. / Silla de oropel / para su mujer.)'. Here he seems to be both alluding to and playing with the children's song 'Coche de oro para el moro, coche de plata para la infanta'. In the poem the stronger contrast of 'oropel' with 'oro' suggests that the wife will be a distinctly second-class citizen.

that she will never have children she also sees herself as dried up. Her pain — 'agonía' — arises both from the dissonance between her actual age and the fact that her child-bearing years have ended before they began, and from her coming face to face with this inescapable fact.

From another, closely related perspective, the plot of the play could simply be summarized as Yerma waiting for something to happen (and then in Act III, trying to make something happen, by resorting to Dolores and attending the *romería*). Lorca exploits the bisemy of the Spanish verb *esperar*, meaning both to wait and to hope: while Yerma waits, she also hopes, and she tries to keep her hopes up while she waits. In the very first exchange between Juan and Yerma, he counters her anxieties with the cliché '¡Hay que esperar!' (35), and the Vieja consoles and encourages Yerma: 'No pases tristeza. Espera en firme. Eres muy joven todavía' (52). Even when the noun makes the meaning clear (*espera*, waiting; *esperanza*, hope), the one tends to imply the other. Thus in Yerma's conversation with María, she justifies her impatience with precise chronological references that she obviously has at her fingertips: 'Es así. Claro que todavía es tiempo. Elena tardó tres años, y otras antiguas, del tiempo de mi madre, mucho más, pero dos años y veinte días, como yo, es demasiada espera' (41). And when Juan goes off to irrigate, Yerma asks '¿Te espero?' (62), meaning something like 'Shall I expect you?', 'Shall I wait up for you?', but of course if Juan does not return and spend the night with her, Yerma cannot entertain the slightest hope of conceiving. Towards the end of the play, the stress seems to shift more towards hope and, by implication, its opposite, despair: 'YERMA: Cada vez tengo más deseos y menos esperanzas' (85); 'YERMA: ¿Y no podré esperarlo [tu hijo]? JUAN: No' (122; *16*; *24*, p. 249; *45*, p. 253).

As a result, Yerma feels hemmed in and trapped (*2*, p. 25); the very limited solutions to her problem do not work, and she rules out other remedies as beyond the pale. This feeling of powerlessness and frustration makes her continuously anxious and ill-at-ease, as well as causing her great emotional pain, which she nevertheless manages to hold in most of the time: 'Vivo sumisa a ti y lo que sufro lo guardo pegado a mis carnes' (78); 'Pero yo no duermo, yo no puedo dormir' (79); '¡Ay, qué prado de pena!' (82); 'la rama de mi angustia' (83); 'MARÍA: ¡Qué trabajos estás pasando, qué trabajos[!]' (86). However, to Juan's way of thinking Yerma is just overly stubborn, but she rejects his advice and justifies her attitude of quiet resistance:

> JUAN: Con este achaque vives alocada, sin pensar en lo que debías, y te empeñas en meter la cabeza por una roca.
>
> YERMA: Roca que es una infamia que sea roca, porque debía ser un canasto de flores y agua dulce.
>
> JUAN: Estando a tu lado no se siente más que inquietud, desasosiego. En último caso debes resignarte.
>
> YERMA: Yo he venido a estas cuatro paredes para no resignarme. Cuando tenga la cabeza atada con un pañuelo para que no se me abra la boca, y las manos bien amarradas dentro del ataúd, en esa hora me habré resignado.
>
> JUAN: Entonces, ¿qué quieres hacer?
>
> YERMA: Quiero beber agua y no hay vaso ni agua; quiero subir al monte y no tengo pies; quiero bordar mis enaguas y no encuentro los hilos. (80)

In this important exchange, we see that although Yerma feels profoundly thwarted, she asserts her determination to maintain her stance of quiet defiance in the face of her unsatisfactory life until the very end. Later, Yerma swaps the image of rock for a wall, adding an ominous prediction: 'Cuando salía por mis claveles me tropecé con el muro. ¡Ay! ¡Ay! Es en ese muro donde tengo que estrellar mi cabeza' (104). Building on these images of confinement, of unbreachable boundaries — women inside their houses, four walls, tomb, rock, wall — she next figures herself as inextricably trapped within a well: 'Dejarme libre siquiera la voz. Ahora que voy entrando en lo más oscuro del pozo. (*Se levanta.*) Dejar que de mi

cuerpo salga siquiera esta cosa hermosa y que llene el aire' (105).
The imagery used here picks up an earlier comment by Yerma —
'De mí sé decir que he aborrecido el agua de estos pozos' (89) —
and we can grasp the importance of the figurative sense of this
(especially given that we know that the village has a river and
fountains: chapters 2 and 5). Furthermore, the voice that comes out
of her body also connects with an earlier reference to 'lo que puede
salir relumbrando de mi pecho' (51).

In what is one of the most crucial speeches in the whole play,
Yerma once more describes her predicament, in simple and poignant
terms:

> Yo pienso que tengo sed y no tengo libertad. Yo quiero
> tener a mi hijo en los brazos para dormir tranquila y,
> óyelo bien y no te espantes de lo que digo: aunque yo
> supiera que mi hijo me iba a martirizar después y me iba
> a odiar y me iba a llevar de los cabellos por las calles,
> recibiría con gozo su nacimiento, porque es mucho
> mejor llorar por un hombre vivo que nos apuñala, que
> llorar por este fantasma sentado año tras año encima de
> mi corazón. (97–98)

We are already familiar with the idea that she has wants and desires
but no means to satisfy them, that she cannot be as she would like to
be, but now the term 'libertad' resonates that much more strongly
with those previous images of entrapment and confinement. Furthermore, Yerma introduces another idea here, and tells the Vieja 1ª that
she would prefer to live with something concrete (a child) rather than
something abstract (her longings), even if she knew in advance that
the son would turn on her later; if life is going to be painful either
way, it is much better to have something tangible to hold on to.

As time passes, it is entirely understandable that her feelings of
helplessness and of irritation and frustration at that helplessness
continue to grow:

YERMA: Yo no debo tener manos de madre.

MARÍA: ¿Por qué me dices eso?

YERMA (*Se levanta.*): Porque estoy harta, porque estoy
harta de tenerlas y no poderlas usar en cosa propia. (84)

In conversation with Víctor, Yerma hints at all that she has bottled
up inside:

YERMA: Siendo zagalón me llevaste una vez en brazos;
¿no recuerdas? Nunca se sabe lo que va a pasar.

VÍCTOR: Todo cambia.

YERMA: Algunas cosas no cambian. Hay cosas
encerradas detrás de los muros que no pueden cambiar
porque nadie las oye.

VÍCTOR: Así es.
[…]

YERMA: Pero que si salieran de pronto y gritaran,
llenarían el mundo.

VÍCTOR: No se adelantaría nada. La acequia por su
sitio, el rebaño en el redil, la luna en el cielo y el hombre
con su arado. (90–91)

Interestingly, Víctor's responses are generally little more than
clichés, but these range widely, from a 'things change' attitude to
one of 'a place for everything and everything in its place'. Furthermore, it is perhaps significant that he (at least) does not believe that
unleashing those 'cosas encerradas' that Yerma darkly alludes to
would move things forward in any profitable way.

After the momentary attempt at reconciliation during the scene
in Dolores's house — '(*En un arranque y abrazándose a su
marido.*)' (103), Yerma lapses into a state of despondency and
defeatism. She recasts once more that doomed conflict of wanting
and being prevented, concedes that she cannot fight impossible odds,

and renounces even the freedom of her voice that she had pleaded for only moments earlier:

> Una cosa es querer con la cabeza y otra cosa es que el cuerpo, ¡maldito sea el cuerpo!, no nos responda. ¡Está escrito y no me voy a poner a luchar a brazo partido con los mares! ¡Ya está! ¡Que mi boca se quede muda! (106)

Here too we find the most explicit reference up to this point of the concept of fate — '¡Está escrito[!]', of the idea that Yerma is somehow destined to be childless, though the notion is already there inherent in her much earlier complaints about the unfairness of life. Once mentioned, the concept soon returns, in the related idea of a curse:

> VIEJA: Mira qué maldición ha venido a caer sobre tu hermosura.
>
> YERMA: Una maldición. Un charco de veneno sobre las espigas. (117)

and in Yerma's grim resolve to see her lot and her life through to the end: 'Por el camino que voy seguiré' (118).

The state of physical collapse into which Yerma falls at the end of Act III, Scene i is confirmed in the following scene, both by María: 'Ella ha estado un mes sin levantarse de la silla' (109) and by the stage directions: '(YERMA *está abatida y no habla*.)' (116), '(YERMA *da muestras de cansancio…*' (116). At the same time it is obvious that her mental activity has not ceased, despite her immobility and silence: 'MARÍA: Le tengo miedo. Tiene una idea que no sé cuál es, pero desde luego es una idea mala' (109); '(YERMA *da muestras […] de persona a la que una idea fija le quiebra la cabeza*.)' (116). This is truly the calm before the storm.

Her near-mutism is finally broken by the encounter with the Vieja at the *romería*; the Vieja tries to engage her in conversation, but her continuing mental turmoil is evident: '(*Pausa. Llevándose las manos a la frente*.) ¡Ay!' (117). Yerma interacts with her in brief phrases until she is finally provoked by what, to her mind, is a demeaning and offensive offer, that she go and live with the Vieja and her son and have a child with him. Here Yerma reasserts her sense of pride, of selfhood and identify, she recovers that defiant attitude noted earlier, and touches once more on how undeserved, how unjust her plight really is:

> ¿Has pensado en serio que yo me pueda doblar a otro hombre? ¿Que yo vaya a pedirle lo que es mío como una esclava? Conóceme, para que nunca me hables más. Yo no busco. (118)

Having made herself subject to one man ('vivo sumisa a ti', 78) she is not going to make the mistake a second time. Implicitly Yerma suggests that the simple ability to have children should be possessed by all women, including her — 'lo que es mío', that it is, or should be, a natural right, and with a truly visceral force to her indignation she rejects the idea that at this stage, after all that she has been through, she should have to make further efforts to achieve childbirth: it would be demeaning for her to have to seek out and request from another (man) something that should by rights already be hers (*2*, p. 36; *19*, pp. 200–01, 210; *21*, pp. 74–75; *27*, pp. 159–60). Yerma wants things on her own terms: to have bent ('doblar') her will, her entire being to one man is already much more of a compromise than she is comfortable with, and she resents it; the very act of compromise is odious to her, because she values her integrity, her wholeness, and the further compromise involved in submitting to a second man is therefore simply out of the question.[33]

Yerma also makes it abundantly clear that the Vieja's offer is too little, too late; the anguish that she now feels, after these years of suffering, is something much broader and all-encompassing that has somehow moved on to a higher and more general plane of being (*4*,

---

[33]There may be a sexual innuendo, too, in the phrase 'doblar a otro hombre', which would make the notion even more repugnant to Yerma: she no more wants to have to bend her will than to have to bend her body.

pp. 17–18; *26*, p. 136; *39*, p. 30; *51*, p. 123). This she expresses with a remarkable density of figurative language, combining in one extraordinary sentence many of the symbols that run through the text of the play: 'Yo soy como un campo seco donde caben arando mil pares de bueyes, y lo que tú me das en un pequeño vaso de agua de pozo. Lo mío es dolor que ya no está en las carnes' (118). The ploughshare on the plough (pulled by a team of oxen) is a traditional phallic symbol, penetrating the surface of 'mother earth'; afterwards, the ploughman goes along and scatters the seeds into the open furrows (*50*, p. 49). The degree and intensity of Yerma's suffering is suggested by the '*mil* pares de bueyes' that would fit into the one field that she says she is, and by the contrast of this immensity with 'un *pequeño* vaso de agua de *pozo*'. A broadly similar idea — though the imagery works in an almost opposite direction — is also suggested in Yerma's last exchange with Juan, where to his recrimination 'Que tengo el amargor en la garganta', she replies: 'Y yo en los huesos' (120); her pain is not skin-deep, but rather in the very marrow of her being.

Yerma's increasing frustration and suffering are matched by a growing conviction of the senselessness of the world and a feeling of alienation from physical reality (*1*, p. 28). At first Yerma tries to retain her sense of connectedness to things: 'Muchas veces salgo descalza al patio para pisar la tierra, no sé por qué' (41), and a similar activity is implied by Lavandera 5ª: 'Estas machorras son así […] les gusta […] andar descalzas por esos ríos' (65). She strives to remain like the Lavandera 4ª, who asserts 'Me gusta el olor de las ovejas […] Olor de lo que una tiene. Como me gusta el olor del fango rojo que trae el río por el invierno' (69). But she does not succeed; to Juan's imputation that 'no eres una mujer verdadera' she replies: 'Yo no sé quién soy' (81).[34] Finally, as her desperation mounts, she tells Dolores:

---

[34]Note that Juan is referring not to her barrenness, but rather to her disregard for his social reputation.

> Lo tendré porque lo tengo que tener. O no entiendo el
> mundo. A veces, cuando ya estoy segura de que jamás,
> jamás…, me sube como una oleada de fuego por los pies
> y se me quedan vacías todas las cosas, y los hombres que
> andan por la calle y los toros y las piedras me parecen
> como cosas de algodón. Y me pregunto: ¿para qué
> estarán ahí puestos? (97)

In this important speech it is self-evident that her disconnection is
virtually complete: she perceives other people, animals and things as
insubstantial puffs of cotton wool, and she can see no reason for
anything — the world has lost its meaning, its logic, its
purposefulness, and so here Yerma experiences pure contingency (*3*,
pp. 26–27; *12*, pp. 29–30; *32*, p. 20).

Yerma's way of living her life and her attitudes toward it stand
out not only because she is the protagonist and they are necessarily
in the foreground of our attention, but also because they are
presented against an array of other lifestyles and perspectives. Juan's
priorities and values have already been studied (chapter 2), but he
also has advice for Yerma and opinions about her stance, such as
when he suggests: 'En último caso debes resignarte' (80). Although
these opinions can be observed and intuited in his behaviour and
comments throughout the play, they are laid out most explicitly in
the final conversation with Yerma:

> JUAN: Ha llegado el último minuto de resistir este
> continuo lamento por cosas oscuras, fuera de la vida, por
> cosas que están en el aire.
>
> YERMA (*Con asombro dramático.*): Fuera de la vida
> dice. En el aire dice.
>
> JUAN: Por cosas que no han pasado y ni tú ni yo
> dirigimos.
>
> YERMA (*Violenta.*): ¡Sigue! ¡Sigue!

JUAN: Por cosas que a mí no me importan. ¿Lo oyes?
Que a mí no me importan. Ya es necesario que te lo diga.
A mí me importa lo que tengo entre las manos. Lo que
veo por mis ojos.

YERMA (*Incorporándose de rodillas, desesperada.*):
Así, así. [...] ¡No le importa! ¡Ya lo he oído!

JUAN (*Acercándose.*): Piensa que tenía que pasar así.
[...] Muchas mujeres serían felices de llevar tu vida.
[...]

JUAN (*Fuerte.*): [...] a ver si de una vez vives ya
tranquila!
[...]

JUAN: [...] ¡Resígnate!
[...]

JUAN: Y a vivir en paz. Uno y otro, con suavidad, con
agrado. (120–23)

Juan's attitude, then, is pragmatic and focussed on the here and now.
He wants Yerma to resign herself to her lot, because it is something
entirely beyond their control, and he points out that by most people's
criteria her life is not that bad a one: they have a good material
standard of living within the village, he is solicitous of her material
needs, not having children has a number of distinct advantages, and
they could enjoy each other's companionship.

Juan's viewpoint is essentially seconded by a number of the
other characters. At several different points throughout the play
María likewise offers an outlook that could be characterized as
passive, resigned, almost quietistic in nature: 'Nadie puede quejarse
de estas cosas' (41); 'No te quejes' (83); 'Pero tienes otras cosas. Si
me oyeras, podrías ser feliz' (84); 'Cada criatura tiene su razón' (85);
'Tiene hijos la que los tiene que tener' (109). The Lavandera 2ª
provides a trenchant analysis of the troubles in the Juan-Yerma
household: 'Todo esto son cuestiones de gente que no tiene
conformidad con su sino' (67), and she is echoed by the Vieja 1ª:

'Está bien que una casada quiera hijos, pero si no los tiene, ¿por qué ese ansia de ellos? Lo importante de este mundo es dejarse llevar por los años' (97). Even Víctor, while not judging Yerma, seems to be passive and accepting: 'Todos los campos son iguales. [...] Es todo lo mismo. Las mismas ovejas tienen la misma lana' (89). Besides Yerma, only the rebellious and worldly-wise Muchacha 2ª rejects the status quo and the received wisdom of her elders. She too wants to assert her right to act as she sees fit, to go and come as she please, and she offers a grim diagnosis of the overall situation when she tells Yerma that just about everybody is stuck inside their houses doing what they don't want to do:

> Yo tengo diecinueve años y no me gusta guisar, ni lavar.
> Bueno, pues todo el día he de estar haciendo lo que no
> me gusta. ¿Y para qué? ¿Qué necesidad tiene mi marido
> de ser mi marido? Porque lo mismo hacíamos de novios
> que ahora. Tonterías de los viejos. (55)

> Yo te puedo decir lo único que he aprendido en la vida:
> toda la gente está metida dentro de sus casas haciendo lo
> que no les gusta. Cuánto mejor se está en medio de la
> calle. Ya voy al arroyo, ya subo a tocar las campanas, ya
> me tomo un refresco de anís. (55)

There are, though, two major differences between the Muchacha 2ª and Yerma: Yerma is much more accepting of the established social *mores* and wants to work within them, whereas Muchacha 2ª would happily throw them off, and Yerma pins her hopes of happiness and fulfilment on motherhood, whereas Muchacha 2ª clearly enjoys sexual relations with her fiancé/husband.

Given Yerma's predicament, and given the kind of community in which she lives, one might have expected that religious belief would have played an important role in the action, perhaps in setting her affliction within the context of the inscrutability of God's design, and certainly in offering solace and support. But this is generally not the case; religion does not figure as a prominent factor in village life and, when mentioned at all, it is sometimes presented in a negative light (*11*, p. 78; *14*, p. 90; *47*, p. 160).

Overall, Yerma would appear to hold a conventional belief in God, one which in all likelihood she inherited from her family and continues to espouse largely because it is part of the fabric of the social order (chapter 3). While she does not seem to take much comfort in religion, nonetheless she utters certain set phrases, such as 'que Dios me ampare' (52), and readily endorses Víctor's good wishes with '¡Dios te oiga!' (93). As for other characters in the play, despite the decidedly heterodox practices of Dolores and her assistants in the cemetery, almost all of them implicitly believe in God and His power:

> YERMA: ¿Y no le pasó nada [a la mujer mendicante]?
>
> DOLORES: ¿Qué le iba a pasar? Dios es Dios. (96)
>
> VIEJA 1ª: …mientras esperas la gracia de Dios, debes ampararte en el amor de tu marido. (98)
>
> VIEJA 1ª: No es nadie. Anda con Dios. (101)

The two Cuñadas who come to live with Juan and Yerma are depicted as *beatas* and used to be in charge of looking after the local church (64), and some of the Mujeres at the *romería* are equally devout:

> VIEJA (*Con sorna.*): ¿Habéis bebido ya el agua santa?
>
> MUJER 1ª: Sí.
>
> VIEJA: Y ahora, a ver a ése.
>
> MUJER 2ª: Creemos en él. (108)

On the other hand, attending church services is never once mentioned in the text, nor does a parish priest ever appear among the secondary characters. Inasmuch as she considers her life a waste, in that she is infertile, Yerma says that she feels somehow abandoned by God: 'La mujer del campo que no da hijos es inútil como un manojo de espinos, ¡y hasta mala!, a pesar de que yo sea de este desecho dejado de la mano de Dios' (84). Furthermore, she has distinct doubts about seeking help from Dolores:

> YERMA (*Con desaliento.*): ¡No sé por qué he venido!
>
> DOLORES: ¿Te arrepientes?
>
> YERMA: ¡No! (100)

and almost identical reservations about attending the *romería*:

> VIEJA: (*Entra* YERMA.) ¡Tú! (YERMA *está abatida y no habla.*) Dime, ¿para qué has venido?
>
> YERMA: No sé.
>
> VIEJA: ¿No te convences? (116)

But it is the Vieja who most unequivocally puts forward a point of view oppositional to religion, and strives to convince Yerma that she is right:

> VIEJA: A otra mujer serena yo le hablaría. A ti, no. Soy vieja y sé lo que digo.
>
> YERMA: Entonces, que Dios me ampare.
>
> VIEJA: Dios, no. A mí no me ha gustado nunca Dios. ¿Cuándo os vais a dar cuenta de que no existe? Son los hombres los que te tienen que amparar.
>
> YERMA: Pero ¿por qué me dices eso?, ¿por qué?
>
> VIEJA (*Yéndose.*): Aunque debía haber Dios, aunque fuera pequeñito, para que mandara rayos contra los hombres de simiente podrida que encharcan la alegría de los campos. (52)

Later on, the most cynical interpretation of the activities at the *romería* is again that presented by the Vieja:

> VIEJA: Venís a pedir hijos al Santo y resulta que cada
> año vienen más hombres solos a esta romería. ¿Qué es lo
> que pasa? (*Ríe.*)
>
> MUJER 1ª: ¿A qué vienes aquí, si no crees?
> [...]
>
> MUJER 1ª: ¡Que Dios te perdone!
> (*Entran.*)
>
> VIEJA (*Con sarcasmo.*): ¡Que te perdone a ti! (108)

These various viewpoints serve to frame Yerma's participation with several other Mujeres in a procession and prayer that form part of the devotional practices that are performed outside the chapel on the mountainside (110–11): '(*Se oyen voces. Entra* YERMA *con seis* MUJERES *que van a la iglesia. Van descalzas y llevan cirios rizados. Empieza el anochecer.*)' (110). We know that the Mujeres are sincere in their veneration for the local saint, and the scepticism that Yerma voices a little while later to the Vieja (116) is nowhere to be detected in Yerma's poetic supplication: 'Escucha a la penitente / de tu santa romería' (111). Of course, we never come to know exactly what is in Yerma's mind. Does she become discouraged at Dolores's house and again at the shrine because of doubts about the legitimacy of the proceedings, about the efficacy of prayer in and of itself, or is it the unlikelihood of their potential efficacy in her (extreme) case?

Be this as it may, Yerma's recourse to Dolores 'la conjuradora' and her presence at the *romería* suggest a kind of 'try anything' attitude as part of her increasingly desperate frame of mind. At the same time, these scenes in Act III make it necessary for us to consider two topics both closely related to orthodox religion, namely superstition and paganism. I have already commented on the blend of Christianity and folk belief represented by Dolores (chapter 6), and it is not surprising that superstition can thrive in this village where strong Christian faith seems to be in a minority, observational practices are invisible, and a few are complete non-believers. Furthermore, given the environment in which the villagers live, we can readily understand the development of a kind of pantheistic paganism based on the natural world that exists syncretistically with Christianity (*23*, p. 357). The local saint is held to help barren women, and so it is not that much of a leap to the 'dos máscaras populares' who incarnate the principles of male and female and heterosexual union (112).[35] Lorca emphasizes their telluric quality by stressing that 'no son grotescas de ningún modo, sino de gran belleza y con un sentido de pura tierra' (112). Hence the cry of the Niños that greets the arrival of the masks is, strictly speaking, incorrect, but at the same time it points to the underlying syncretic connections: '¡El demonio y su mujer! ¡El demonio y su mujer!' (112; *35*, p. 243); likewise the last four lines of Macho's sexually explicit song are, strikingly, a reprise of Yerma's prayer (110–11, 116; see chapter 4).

Now, if we explore ways of extrapolating from the predicament that Yerma finds herself in and the tense struggle in which she engages, it rapidly becomes apparent that they configure a coherent and extended sequence of core existentialist ideas. Yerma is a *campesina* with an intuitive grasp of the world rather than an intellectual one, and so, as in many other of Lorca's plays, she experiences her life more on a gut level than a cerebral one. As Lorca stated in an interview: 'Deliberadamente he cuidado de eliminar todo producto de elaboración mental. No me interesa. Tengo dos obras que no doy por demasiado intelectuales. Entrego ésta al fresco instinto, al gemido más primario de la naturaleza' (197). However, this is no impediment to our teasing out the broader, more abstract ramifications of the situation (*4*, pp. 18–19; *32*, p. 26). Yerma's lot, then, leads us to the following reflexions. Nature is neutral and indifferent, it is neither a beneficent 'Mother Nature' nor

---

[35]'Popular' is the adjective derived from 'pueblo', the people, and so it is clearly indicated that the representation here of these two fundamental principles derives from the popular imagination.

a deliberately cruel or vengeful nature. Its laws are fixed and a given; it is nature that determines that there is a fixed span to the existence of all living things (*42*, pp. 92–93). Mankind cannot be held responsible for its own mortality, then, and, furthermore, to many it seems extraordinarily unfair or totally arbitrary that such an absolute limitation should be set on human life and the consciousness that accompanies it. Temporality, of course, goes hand in hand with mortality; time passes and living things age, and it is precisely the awareness of the transitory, fleeting quality of existence that directs attention towards its rapidly approaching end (*16*). Faced by this set of circumstances, people feel trapped and frustrated, because their freedom of action is severely curtailed (*3*, pp. 26–27): there is no way to overcome one's own mortality, and aspirations to transcend the mortal condition are by definition doomed to failure (*42*, pp. 92–94). All these considerations presuppose a lack of religious belief (*47*, p. 160); the Bible holds mankind responsible for its mortal condition, and if there is no God there is also no afterlife, which has been the traditional response to the grim prospect of human mortality. Without God and without ultimate, absolute freedom, the universe takes on a quality of meaninglessness or purposelessness: everything becomes arbitrary and pointless.

Furthermore, the existential dilemma also allows for a kind of recasting or reinterpretation of the classical idea of fate: where in Greek mythology the Moirai (Roman Parcae) were in control, with Klotho presiding over birth, Lachesis over life, and Atropos over death, in the existential version nobody is in control; mankind is destined, is predetermined to die, but that appointed lot has not been appointed by anyone, human, supernatural, or divine (*42*, pp. 91–94). As Yerma herself says: 'Una maldición. Un charco de veneno sobre las espigas' (117); fate is a kind of curse, and it has happened to fall upon her, a woman, just as that 'charco de veneno' might fall on the ears of wheat that are an archetypal part of nature (*1*, p. 22; *4*, p. 10; *14*, p. 89; *23*, p. 359; *34*, p. 228).

This atmosphere of predetermination and inescapability that hangs over the action of the play is intensified further by various techniques of foreshadowing. Thus Yerma imagines the unrelieved

relentlessness of married life: 'Tú y yo seguiremos aquí cada año…'
(33). In conversation with María, still in Act I, Scene i, she confides
her fears: 'Si sigo así, acabaré volviéndome mala' (41) and makes a
dire prediction: 'Cada mujer tiene sangre para cuatro o cinco hijos, y
cuando no los tienen se les vuelve veneno, como me va a pasar a mí'
(42-43). As time passes Yerma's vision of the future seems to be
coming true: 'No, vacía no, porque me estoy llenando de odio' (51);
'Y cada día que pase será peor' (78); and her remark to Víctor, by
itself a simple cliché, acquires new weight in the light of the
denouement: 'Nunca se sabe lo que va a pasar' (90). Finally, in the
last scene, it becomes clear that things must follow their course; the
offer that the Vieja makes to Yerma is not only too little, too late, but
also in some sense a sheer irrelevance, a mere and passing distraction
from what now has to happen: 'El agua no se puede volver atrás, ni
la luna llena sale al mediodía. Vete. Por el camino que voy seguiré'
(118).

There is a wide variety of possible reactions to this ineluctable
situation. Anguish is perhaps the most obvious, arising from the
contemplation of temporality, mortality, the absurdity of existence,
and the inability of the individual to alter any of these (*15*, pp.
126–27). But there are other responses too, ranging from despair and
even suicide, through resignation or apathy, to more defiant or
proactive postures. There is the familiar Sartrian idea of living
making choices, of taking charge of the course of one's life (if not of
one's life itself in more absolute terms), of actively deciding to do A
and not B. There is the broader notion of life as a struggle, picking
up on the etymology of the word agony, and of the very act of
struggling as life-affirming or life-reinforcing.[36] And there is the
prolongation of oneself beyond mortality through one medium or
another: through fame (living on in the memory of others), creation
(living on in things one has made), or procreation (living on in one's
children).

---

[36]This connects with the point of view, simply put, that it is better to feel
something, even unpleasant or painful, rather than to feel nothing at all.
When one feels something one knows oneself to be alive; when one feels
nothing, it is a kind of living death.

Within her limited horizons fixed by the village, Yerma has intuitively focussed her attention and energies on procreation, but this — with the most fundamental and profound of tragic ironies — is precisely what is denied her. Life, the play seems to be saying, is like that. People don't get what they want (*2*, p. 17; *12*, p. 23; *40*, p. 69). We have already noted Muchacha 2ª's comment to the effect that 'toda la gente está metida dentro de sus casas haciendo lo que no les gusta' (55), to which we could now add that they are also trapped there inside their houses wanting what they can't or won't get. Human beings want to be immortal, to transcend their earthly limitations, just as Yerma wants a child. The parallel is doubly poignant: human beings in general and Yerma in particular are equally frustrated in what they desire, but also the very object of Yerma's desire is precisely one way, one path, that humans have found that enables them, at least in part, to cheat mortality. To return to my point of departure in this chapter, this last observation is the reason why I see the literal level of the action and the more abstract level of the theme as very close together; it takes only a slight shift of perspective to see Yerma's individual predicament in the broadest of human terms (*12*, p. 31).

If we wish to situate the sequence of ideas that arise from the play within their wider existentialist context, then Unamuno presents himself immediately as the writer and philosopher who is closest in spirit. Paternity is a key motif in the 'Continuación' section of Unamuno's *Cómo se hace una novela* (1927), but he was perhaps even more fascinated by the topic of motherhood and, especially, frustrated motherhood and maternal surrogates. This can be observed in a number of his literary works, most notably the story 'Dos madres' from *Tres novelas ejemplares y un prólogo* (1920), where the protagonist's name is Raquel, the novel *La tía Tula* (1921), and the play originally entitled *Raquel* and subsequently retitled *Raquel encadenada* (1921) (*3*, p. 14; *32*, p. 27 n21). It should be noted that in each instance the plots of these works and their outcomes are substantially different from what happens in *Yerma*. Nonetheless, we have it on the authority of Lorca's brother that after seeing the play performed, 'Unamuno [...] dijo generosamente a Federico [...] que *Yerma* era la obra que a él le hubiese gustado escribir' (*23*, p. 347).

Equally relevant are Unamuno's philosophical essays *Del sentimiento trágico de la vida* (1913) and *La agonía del cristianismo* (1925). The former is centrally concerned with man's hunger for immortality, the inexorable fact of death, and the many reasons to doubt whether immortality can be achieved; it is in this dilemma and the struggle to believe that Unamuno locates that 'tragic sense' of his title (*16*). Furthermore, he considers several ways in which man tries to attain at least a mediated immortality, even though, Unamuno concludes, those paths are compromised and that partial immortality unsatisfactory. His primary examples are artists (writers, painters, sculptors, composers, etc.) who create in order to leave something of themselves behind and to be remembered, and famous men (kings, politicians, generals, etc.) who hope to live on in their deeds and above all — through their fame — in the collective memory (see chapter 3, 'El hambre de inmortalidad'). In *La agonía del cristianismo* Unamuno dedicates chapter 9, 'El padre Jacinto', to a historical figure, the French cleric Father Hyacinthe Loyson. Loyson was preoccupied by what would remain of him in this world after his death; he eventually left the church in order to marry, he married in order to be able to have children, and he wanted to have children in order to perpetuate his flesh. Ironically, Loyson's son Paul predeceased him, but not before he himself had fathered offspring, thereby giving Loyson grandchildren.[37]

Besides Unamuno, at least one critic has sought to relate Lorca's tragedies to the philosophy of Heidegger (*15*), but while Carbonell Basset's suggestions are undoubtedly interesting, I find more points of contact with Schopenhauer, a philosopher whom Lorca almost certainly never read directly, but whose key ideas could easily have filtered through to him, primarily in none other than Unamuno's writings. Yerma's obsessiveness, determination and

---

[37]For more details see Manuel Blanco, *La voluntad de vivir y sobrevivir en Miguel de Unamuno: el deseo del Infinito imposible* (Madrid: ABL Editor / Franciscanos (OFM) Castilla, 1994), which is centred exactly on this topic.

struggle could be viewed through the optic of Schopenhauer's basic concept of the will, which in his definition is a 'striving and mostly unconscious force' (p. 545).[38] More specifically, Schopenhauer views 'the whole of animate nature as forever striving, struggling and competing to live and to further life by producing offspring' (p. 549), a picture of the natural world highly reminiscent of that offered in *Yerma*. Yerma's own all-consuming preoccupation with procreation is close to Schopenhauer's notion of the 'will to life', for 'the drive to reproduce [is] one principal way in which the will to life manifests itself throughout nature' (p. 550), reproduction being, according to Schopenhauer, nature's way of responding to, coping with, or even conquering mortality. However, again much as with Yerma, 'the will to life drives us on through an ever-ramifying set of desires and goals, but we reach no ultimate point or final satisfaction. To have desires unsatisfied is to suffer, [and] to have needs is to be vulnerable to deprivation' (p. 550). Finally, 'it is essential to Schopenhauer's thought that there is no supreme end, no grand design, purpose or meaning. There is no answer to the question why the will wills as it does' (p. 550), a kind of pessimistic nihilism which anticipates the existentialist concepts of contingency and absurdity.

---

[38]Christopher Janaway, 'Schopenhauer, Arthur (1788–1860)', in *Routledge Encyclopedia of Philosophy*, ed. Edward Craig (London: Routledge, 1998), pp. 545–54.

8. The Denouement

We should now be in a position to consider one final but crucial issue with respect to Yerma: why does she strangle Juan at the very end of the play, and what implications does this extraordinary act have? There are several possible answers to these questions, none of them mutually exclusive, some which have more to do with the particular circumstances, and others which have broader implications. Most obviously, Yerma's frustration boils over, with fatal consequences. We have seen how the action of the play spans several years (chapter 4), how Yerma's longings become ever more intense, exacerbated by the passing of time (chapter 7), and how Juan's attitude remains largely the same: he no more wants children at the end of the play than at the beginning, and the only aspects that really change are his growing concern for his reputation and his increasing irritation with his wife's obsession (chapters 2, 6). Yerma has very few options that she is willing to consider (chapter 6), and although she allows no time for her participation in the *romería* to work, it is clear that she holds out no real hope of ever conceiving a child — the passage of the years has all but extinguished that expectation in her. This point is driven home in the conversation with the Vieja, where the old woman spitefully compares her to 'los cardos del secano, pinchosa, marchita', a crucial, eye-opening moment which Yerma says is 'la primera vez que veo que es verdad' (119). Moments later, in the course of her last exchange with Juan, comes the final straw that provokes Yerma to action.

Juan, too, wants some closure: 'Ha llegado el último minuto de resistir este continuo lamento' (120), but for him it is a question of Yerma needing to exercise her will, shift her focus and accept things as they are. He explains to her that having children or not is completely out of their control, that it does not matter to him, and that to his way of thinking being childless has a number of distinct advantages (120–21). Here he states his standpoint more explicitly and forcefully than ever before, and this openness — echoing that of the Vieja moments before — seems to galvanize Yerma:

> (*Incorporándose de rodillas, desesperada.*): Así, así. Eso es lo que yo quería oír de tus labios. No se siente la verdad cuando está dentro de una misma, pero qué grande y cómo grita cuando se pone fuera y levanta los brazos. (121)

Ignoring Yerma's mocking tones — '¡No le importa! ¡Ya lo he oído!' (121) — and in a moment of something approaching tenderness, Juan draws near her and '(*La abraza para incorporarla.*)' (121). Jolted by his frank words into a more acute realization of her situation, and at the same time increasingly overwrought, Yerma questions him about the very basis and origins of their relationship:

> YERMA: ¿Y qué buscabas en mí?
>
> JUAN: A ti misma.
>
> YERMA (*Excitada.*):[39] ¡Eso! Buscabas la casa, la tranquilidad y una mujer. Pero nada más. ¿Es verdad lo que digo?
>
> JUAN: Es verdad. Como todos. (121–22)

Juan readily acknowledges that he entered into their marriage seeking nothing in Yerma but Yerma herself — i.e. that he was not thinking about the child or children that Yerma could give him (that they could have together). He believes that it was entirely normal and acceptable to be looking for what Yerma herself could offer him, as a housekeeper, companion and sexual partner — as Yerma puts it 'la casa, la tranquilidad y una mujer'. But Yerma is horrified that

---

[39]Here this adjective means something like 'agitated', 'worked up'.

Juan's expectations went no further than this, and that he was never able to empathize with her desires:

> YERMA: ¿Y lo demás? ¿Y tu hijo?
> [...]
>
> YERMA: ¿Y nunca has pensado en él cuando me has visto desearlo?
>
> JUAN: Nunca. (122)

In the face of this, she seeks final confirmation — reconfirmation, really — that they will never have a child together:

> YERMA: ¿Y no podré esperarlo?
>
> JUAN: No.
>
> YERMA: Ni tú.
>
> JUAN: Ni yo tampoco. (122)

As ever unperceptive, Juan tries yet again to get Yerma to accept her lot and make the best of it, just the two of them together. But Juan's negative response to her question, '¿Y no podré esperarlo?', is still ringing in her ears, connecting as it does with the implications of the home truths that she has just heard from the Vieja, and whose defining adjective she now repeats. Never have Juan and Yerma been talking more at cross purposes:

> JUAN: ¡Resígnate!
>
> YERMA: ¡Marchita!
>
> JUAN: Y a vivir en paz. Uno y otro, con suavidad, con agrado. (122–23).

While Juan is asking Yerma to resign herself once and for all and move on, Yerma's exclamatory response makes it abundantly clear that this is not something that she can just put behind her, as Juan's subsequent remarks would seem to suggest she should do. And then, to make matters worse, in an appallingly ill-timed advance that reveals, yet again, Juan's acute lack of understanding of Yerma, he moves to embrace and then kiss her, mirror-imaging Yerma's advance to him in Act I, Scene i — '(YERMA *abraza y besa al marido tomando ella la iniciativa.*)' (35):

> JUAN: ¡Abrázame!
>
> (*La abraza.*)
>
> YERMA: ¿Qué buscas?
>
> JUAN: A ti te busco. Con la luna estás hermosa.
>
> YERMA: Me buscas como cuando te quieres comer una paloma.
>
> JUAN: Bésame... así.
>
> YERMA: Eso nunca. Nunca.
>
> (YERMA *da un grito y aprieta la garganta de su esposo. Éste cae hacia atrás. Le aprieta la garganta hasta matarle.*) (123)

Juan has been drinking (117), he has no doubt been stimulated by the erotic pagan song and dance and all manner of licentious goings-on in the vicinity of the chapel (chapter 3), and apparently spurred by his vision of the future life they could have together — 'Uno y otro, con suavidad, con agrado' — he experiences a moment of physical attraction for his wife and likely underneath that a pang of simple sexual desire (*7*, p. 464; *35*, p. 243; *38*, p. 70). Both of them are kneeling or sitting on the ground (122) within that 'tienda rústica' formed by blankets (107), to which Yerma has returned after her conversation with the Vieja (119–20) and which may recall, ironically, the 'chocita' of the opening lullaby (31). Juan gives Yerma a passionate kiss, probably a 'French kiss' ('Bésame... así') (*38*, pp. 72–74), and he asks his wife to reciprocate, to take her cue from his example. But rather than becoming aroused, Yerma is immediately repulsed, because he seeks her and nothing more, because he focusses solely on their possible physical pleasure, and this exactly at that moment when she has come to a full, conscious recognition of her present and future barrenness (*38*, pp. 70–71, 74, 78). Strictly speaking, and from a doctrinal point of view, Juan is within his husbandly rights, for Paul enjoins 'defraud ye not one the other' (I Corinthians 7:5), and the exercise of conjugal relations is licit even when for 'natural reasons either of time or of certain defects, new life cannot be brought forth' (chapter 3). But the point is moot, for in a sudden burst of fury Yerma closes her hands around Juan's throat and throttles him to death. Juan has been exhausting himself in the fields for years (32–33, 76), while Yerma has assumed masculine tasks (85; *48*, pp. 27, 31, 33), and so the proposition that she is physically capable of overpowering and killing him is plausible enough, given what we know of both of them and the widely-held notion that people can be endowed with bursts of great short-term strength in extreme and threatening situations.

It is a satisfying artistical effect that Yerma should use her bare hands to perform the deed rather than if she were to attack Juan with some weapon lying conveniently close by. There are in addition a number of symbolic implications associated with the murder and the manner in which it is carried out. For instance, Yerma tells María that 'Yo no debo tener manos de madre' (84), and later exclaims that '¡Y es inútil que me retuerza las manos!' (105), the first an ill-tempered aside, the second a temporary admission of defeat, both of which, retrospectively, acquire much greater significance. Also, Yerma has now definitively silenced Juan's voice (located metonymically in the throat), just as he had repeatedly tried to silence hers, most notably in Dolores's house (105; *51*, pp. 111–12). There may well be an echo too of the 'niño [que] lloraba como ahogado' (60) that Yerma thinks she hears when she is talking with Víctor: 'ahogado' has a figurative sense of stifled or muffled — that is, the sound of the child's crying is faint, but *ahogar* as a transitive verb means to drown, to choke, to asphyxiate, so that strangulation is, symbolically speaking, more than appropriate for Juan (*49*, pp. 272–73).[40]

Now, as we have seen, Yerma has never been at all interested in sex with her husband, that is, in sex for its own sake, but rather solely as a necessary intermediate step (might she say a necessary evil?) towards motherhood. While she was much more accepting of this situation early on in the marriage (cf. Act I, Scene i), her tolerance has been eroded by the passing years until there is none left at all, and she can bear the situation no longer. Juan simply does not understand Yerma, he does not understand her way of thinking, and so he makes these blunders, the last one of which costs him his life. But Yerma is repulsed by Juan's attitude and advances, I would argue, for a number of additional reasons beyond her deep-rooted aversion to eroticism. First, she comes to a full realization of how far apart she and Juan are in terms of envisaging the other's position or empathizing with their feelings; there is no mutual comprehension here, no togetherness in the face of adversity. Next, Yerma experiences Juan's physical desire for her as nothing more than his self-centred need to satisfy a basic appetite, like thirst, or in his case hunger — 'como cuando te quieres comer una paloma'. Furthermore, as the imagery clearly shows, she perceives this situation as very threatening, as if he were going not only to use her but to consume her (*8*, p. 59 n12; *38*, pp. 78–79). Of course, one's sense of individual identity can be reduced or even temporarily engulfed in the sexual act, and this is precisely the only thing that Yerma has left to hang on to — she will not countenance submerging herself, her selfhood, in marital intercourse when its purpose is pleasure and not procreation (*20*, p. 26; *21*, p. 72; *45*, p. 254). Finally, Yerma is likewise resolute in refusing to give up her obsession, her struggle; if she is frustrated in her desire to have a child, then the only sense of self and self-worth that she retains is located in the defiant (if hopeless) attitude that she adopts (*14*, pp.

---

[40]Notice too that this denouement exactly reverses the murder of the wife by the husband found at the end of several well-known Golden Age plays (principally by Calderón), the slaying being motivated most frequently by a supposed stain on the husband's honour (*4*, p. 10; *35*, p. 238).

90–91). As she says: 'Yo he venido a estas cuatro paredes para no resignarme. Cuando tenga la cabeza atada con un pañuelo para que no se me abra la boca, y las manos bien amarradas dentro del ataúd, en esa hora me habré resignado' (80); to resign oneself — as Juan wishes her to do — before that final moment would be to bring about the living death that she is determined not to accept (78).

What Yerma says and how she reacts on realizing that she has actually killed Juan needs to be set in the context of attitudes expressed at several other points in the play. Yerma's description of how she viewed and interacted with Juan is telling:

Pues el primer día que me puse novia con él ya pensé…
en los hijos. Y me miraba en sus ojos. Sí, pero era para
verme muy chica, muy manejable, como si yo misma
fuera hija mía. (50)

…mi hijo. Yo me entregué a mi marido por él, y me sigo
entregando para ver si llega… (51)

Acabaré creyendo que yo misma soy mi hijo. (85)

When Yerma looks into Juan's eyes, instead of seeing Juan, rather she sees herself reflected back in miniature, suggesting that if Juan is interested in Yerma only for herself, Yerma is interested in Juan only as an agent for her impregnation (a point made explicitly in the second quotation), and also that she thinks of her future child as a kind of miniature version of herself (a notion that is developed in the third quotation), and a version that can easily be adapted to her own purposes and ends ('muy manejable'). There is also an element of Narcissism here: Yerma is self-absorbed, and when looking into the 'pools' of Juan's eyes, instead of seeing him, instead of seeing into him through these windows of the soul, rather she stays resolutely on the surface, and sees herself reflected back. Furthermore, it is no coincidence that Narcissism is by definition both sterile and deathly (*9*; see *51*, p. 109).

Yerma's disagreement with Juan on the goals of marriage, her distaste for sexual relations, and the concept of self-prolongation in childbearing come together to produce an extreme sentiment, a kind of longing for the possibility of human parthenogenesis: 'yo sé que los hijos nacen del hombre y de la mujer. ¡Ay, si los pudiera tener yo sola!' (98–99). Although their relevance is not so immediately obvious, this set of ideas also informs the following lines:

> YERMA: No me apartes y quiere conmigo.
>
> JUAN: ¡Quita!
>
> YERMA: Mira que me quedo sola. Como si la luna se
> buscara ella misma por el cielo. ¡Mírame! (*Lo mira.*)
> (104)

The exchange in question occurs in Dolores's house when Yerma makes a brief attempt to spark some life into their husband-wife relationship, an effort that is unsuccessful, miscued and quite possibly ill-conceived. The moon derives its light from the sun; the white light that is visible is reflected light (chapter 5). As demonstrated above, Yerma (the moon) sees herself/her child reflected in the eyes of Juan (the sun).[41] By implication, Yerma requests the heat of Juan's gaze/physical passion to bring life and warmth to the moon (Yerma), but she is rebuffed and pushed away. However, the image itself may be in a sense self-defeating. The moon depends on the sun, but Yerma chafes bitterly at her analogous dependency on Juan. The moon is by definition cold, sterile and lifeless (as is the barren woman who has been named Yerma), and the light with which it seems to shine is actually an illusion. As Yerma says, she is left alone to seek herself or a prolongation of herself, but this latter can only be a reflection of a reflection, insubstantial and intangible. Metaphorically speaking, then, by choosing this image Yerma confirms her sterility and her self-regarding isolation.

---

[41]St John's Eve — la víspera de San *Juan* — coincides more or less with the date of the summer solstice: see *35*, p. 247.

Immediately after strangling Juan, Yerma cries out to a group of onlookers at the *romería* who begin to gather round in order to find out what has happened: '¿Qué queréis saber? No os acerquéis, porque he matado a mi hijo. ¡Yo misma he matado a mi hijo!' (124). Although she can imagine herself as her own offspring and even envisages being able to self-procreate, the primary sense of her comments here does not have to do with Yerma somehow seeing Juan as her own child. Rather the striking phrase is the product of an ellipsis: Yerma knows that a man and a woman, for her, strictly speaking, a husband and a wife, are necessary to conceive a baby; in killing her husband Juan she has eliminated all possibility of her ever having a child, and hence she has killed all hope of her future, unborn offspring (*34*, p. 235; *49*, p. 276).

But at the same time there are other, different resonances in this scene, which do indeed relate to metaphorical redefinitions of Yerma and Juan's relationship. For instance, if we do take Yerma's words literally for a moment — '¡Yo misma he matado a mi hijo!', we may remember her offering Juan a glass of milk in the very opening moments of the play (32), and also her subsequent, repeated fantasies about breast-feeding her newborn infant (36, 82, 97; *31*, p. 13; *50*, p. 45). What we have here, then, are — figuratively speaking — a mourning mother and a dead child, a situation which within the context of Spanish culture is immediately reminiscent of Mary at the foot of the cross on which Christ was crucified. Yerma, the woman who suffered so much for her longing to be a mother, therefore becomes a kind of 'Mater Dolorosa'; inasmuch as she is not cradling Juan's lifeless body (the stage directions, 123, actually call for her to stand up after committing the act), the scene is half way between a true 'Pietà' and the iconic representation of the solitary figure of the mourning Virgin, known precisely in Spanish painting as 'La Soledad' (*19*, pp. 209, 211–12; *35*, p. 244).[42]

---

[42]See James Hall, *Dictionary of Subjects and Symbols in Art*, rev. ed. (London: John Murray, 1979), sections on Virgin Mary and Pietà. This near-archetypal image is even clearer at the end of *Bodas de sangre*: the bodies of the two dead men, the Novio and Leonardo, are described but not on stage,

This religious imagery (very different, one must remember, from the relatively scarce religious content in the plot) has a number of further ramifications (*30*, pp. 35, 40). In the broadest of terms, Yerma's situation is a photographic negative in relation to that of the Virgin Mary. Mary is a virgin who conceives before her marriage to Joseph; Yerma, after her marriage to Juan, is not a virgin yet does not conceive. On the other hand, some of Yerma's attitudes to motherhood (parthenogenesis, becoming her own child) clearly echo the idea of a virgin birth (though again this is what Yerma does not experience) (*30*, p. 38; *38*, p. 75).

The dream sequence at the very opening of the play can therefore be read as a version of the Annunciation, where the shepherd figure deputizes for the archangel Gabriel, but of course it is an Annunciation that is only dreamt by Yerma, and therefore there is no conception or incarnation (*13*, p. 125; *35*, p. 238).[43] Later Yerma's bashful friend María — Mary — tells her that 'a mí me parece que mi niño es un palomo de lumbre que él [mi marido] me deslizó por la oreja' (41). Here we find an allusion to the dove of the Holy Ghost, a dove which is present in representations of the Annunciation, as well as a reference to a tradition of belief that the Holy Spirit entered Mary through the ear, thereby bringing about the Incarnation (*14*, p. 93 n6; *31*, p. 16; *35*, p. 241). Broadly similar suggestions, though in a very different key, can also be detected in Yerma's reproach to Juan at the end of the play that 'me buscas como cuando te quieres comer una paloma' (123). María's relations with her unnamed husband are evidently gentle, tender and loving, though also manifestly sexual, for the 'palomo de lumbre' (note the masculine form of the word here) is, in addition, a clearly phallic symbol, while Yerma sees Juan in an entirely negative light, as

---

and the Madre laments her dead son (and the Novia and the Mujer their dead husbands).

[43]Another way of looking at this would be to say that the shepherd's message in the pantomime has actually been delivered to María, as befits her name, and not to Yerma, as befits hers (*13*, pp. 124–25).

overbearing, lustful, egotistical, devouring and ultimately destructive
(*35*, p. 243).

Yerma may also be compared — and contrasted — with a
number of other women who appear in the Bible and their respective
husbands, namely Sarah and Abraham, Rebekah and Isaac, and
Rachel and Jacob (all in Genesis), Hannah and Elkanah (I Samuel)
(*3*, p. 14), Joachim and Anne, the parents of Mary (*Golden Legend*,
apocryphal Protevangelium: see Hall, *Dictionary*, p. 170), and
Elisabeth and Zacharias, the parents of John the Baptist (Luke) (*31*,
p. 12; *35*, p. 247). In all these cases the wives are barren, often for
long periods of time, in some instances because of their advancing
years but in others for no obvious biological reason (e.g. Hannah:
'because the Lord had shut up her womb', I Samuel 1:6). Most
importantly, in each and every story the women do eventually
become pregnant and bear a child, as does the Virgin Mary. Since
Yerma does not, she must be viewed as their antithesis, a situation
which is in accord with the fact that she finds little comfort in the
church and effectively loses her faith in a benevolent, providential
God (chapter 7). Yerma's problem, then, has no biblical, that is, no
religious, solution — she is indeed part of 'este desecho dejado de la
mano de Dios' (84).

This, however, does not prevent her (and Lorca) from utilizing
a good deal of religious language and imagery — as just noted
above, language and imagery whose resonances would have been
particularly strong for Spanish audiences. Speaking of Juan in Act
III, Scene i, Yerma confesses to Dolores and the Vieja 1ª that: 'No lo
quiero, no lo quiero y, sin embargo, es mi única salvación. Por honra
y por casta. Mi única salvación' (99). Consonant with the notion of
Yerma as a kind of Virgin Mary and Juan as a kind of Christ figure,
here again Juan is cast as both Christ the Saviour and the Christ
child, but with distinctly ambivalent overtones. Juan is Yerma's only
salvation inasmuch as he is her husband, and therefore he is the only
man with whom she is willing to have sexual intercourse in order to
conceive a child, even though, as she says, she does not love him.
There is ellipsis here too, as strictly speaking it would be the child

(in a sense, then, the Christ child), made possible by Juan, who would save Yerma from her barrenness (*30*, p. 35; *35*, p. 238).

A more positive Christological image is also presented in the play, but only really in Yerma's dreams and fantasies, and in the person of a different character, Víctor. Víctor's profession reminds us of Abel, Jacob and Christ the Good Shepherd. Hence part of the meaning of the opening mime:

> *Al levantarse el telón está* YERMA *dormida con un*
> *tabaque de costura a los pies. La escena tiene una*
> *extraña luz de sueño. Un* PASTOR *sale de puntillas*
> *mirando fijamente a Yerma. Lleva de la mano a un*
> NIÑO VESTIDO DE BLANCO. (31)

Just as for the childless Zapatera in Lorca's *La zapatera prodigiosa* lambs are associated with fertility and childbearing (Act I, Scene xii), so too Yerma associates children with a figure that is Víctor, a shepherd and Christ, rolled into one. Víctor's tremendous virility, as least as far as Yerma is concerned, is left in no doubt whatsoever in the extraordinary description that she offers of his singing (an action which itself is associated in the play with conception): 'qué voz tan pujante. Parece un chorro de agua que te llena toda la boca' (58). Yerma fantasizes Víctor, therefore, as the bringer, the enabler, of the child she so wants; he is Jacob to her Rachel, and he is Christ the Good Shepherd, tending to His flock, and truly a saviour of Yerma, but for her in a biological sense rather than a spiritual one.[44] In an alternative reading, already adumbrated above, Víctor serves in place of Gabriel, and hence the child dressed in white now becomes the Christ child, the Lamb of God. A similar motif continues in their next encounter, when Yerma thinks she hears a baby or small child

---

[44]As noted above, the motif of infertility links Yerma's story to Rachel's, but there are important differences. Rachel is like Yerma in that she too is a shepherd's daughter, but she marries another shepherd, Jacob, whereas Yerma marries Juan, essentially a farmer (chapter 2). Hence Víctor becomes the Jacob she should have married, for in the bible story Rachel and Jacob do eventually have children together (*21*, p. 66).

crying close by: 'Muy cerca. Y lloraba como ahogado' (60). As
Víctor cannot hear anything, Yerma is led to conclude that 'serán
ilusiones mías' (60), a comment made all the more poignant by the
fact that 'ilusiones' in Spanish means hopes as well as illusions or
imaginings. All of this adds in turn to the significance of Víctor's
definitive departure at the end of Act II, Scene ii; in Act III all that
he represents is gone for good.

Finally, and rather surprisingly, there is yet other imagery in
the text that portrays Yerma herself as Christ (rather than as the
Virgin Mary) (*3*, p. 33), but the apparent paradox here is perhaps to
be resolved in the notion, already mentioned, of Yerma as her own
offspring (i.e. Yerma as both Mary and Jesus). In particular, it should
be noted that these references again allude exclusively to the this-
worldly suffering of Christ; the stress is very much on the calvary of
earthly existence, and it is perhaps appropriate that the last scene
takes place 'en plena montaña' (107), reminiscent of Golgotha (*25*,
pp. 133–34; *30*, p. 40). In accord with the principal themes of the
play, Christ's death brings with it here no hint or promise of a
heaven:

> YERMA: Yo sabré llevar mi cruz como mejor pueda,
> pero no me preguntes nada. […] Ahora, ahora, déjame
> con mis clavos. (78-79)

> MARÍA: ¡Qué trabajos estás pasando, qué trabajos, pero
> acuérdate de las llagas de Nuestro Señor! (86)

At the end of Act III those travails to which María alludes
prove too much for Yerma, and she finds no conventional solace in
the contemplation of the suffering of the crucified Christ, which
rather she assumes as her own, turning herself into a sort of victim or
martyr (*19*, pp. 202, 209, 211; *25*, p. 140; *31*, p. 18; *50*, p. 51).
Furthermore, Christ as Víctor has disappeared from her world, and
Christ as Juan offers not the slightest hope of salvation. She can go
on no longer, she cannot continue — as it were — to turn the other
cheek, and she explodes in pent-up anger and violence, though
obviously with dire consequences. Those consequences, and how the

denouement affects our reading of the entire play, will be the subject of the next chapter.

9. Tragedy Ancient and Modern

I have yet to comment on the very first words that Yerma utters after she kills her husband:

> Marchita, marchita, pero segura. Ahora sí que lo sé de cierto. Y sola. (*Se levanta. Empieza a llegar gente.*) Voy a descansar sin despertarme sobresaltada para ver si la sangre me anuncia otra sangre nueva. Con el cuerpo seco para siempre. (123–24)

The sentiments expressed here fill in another facet of Yerma's predicament: her suffering is not caused solely by the frustration of her one consuming desire, but also by not knowing for sure, by the hoping against hope that one day she might wake up and discover that she was pregnant. As the years pass, it becomes clear that it is increasingly unlikely that Yerma will ever conceive, but so long as she remains married and engaging in sexual relations with her husband, the possibility, however slim, still exists. Within her self-imposed boundaries, Yerma therefore has two options: continue with the way things are, for another two decades or more until she ceases to be biologically capable of conceiving, or do something now. Unable to countenance the former, and provoked by the Vieja and by Juan, she opts for the latter. But the final tragic irony is that in order to gain respite from the pain occasioned by those last, lingering embers of hope, she must by her own hand eliminate the very precondition of hope itself, namely life with Juan, and furthermore, by so doing, propel her single, lifelong goal into the realm of the irrevocably unattainable. Certainty, then, even though it is a negative certainty — 'marchita, pero segura', offers a kind of relief or repose (*14*, p. 92), but it is bought at an enormous cost. In this regard Yerma also reminds us of the protagonist in the first play of the trilogy. The

Madre in *Bodas de sangre* lives with the constant nagging fear that she will lose her son, the last surviving male in her family; when he is killed she achieves a tranquility that hitherto escaped her:

> Y tranquila. Ya todos están muertos. A media noche dormiré, dormiré sin que ya me aterren la escopeta o el cuchillo. Otras madres se asomarán a las ventanas, azotadas por la lluvia, para ver el rostro de sus hijos. Yo no.[45]

The importance of hope, the way it can make you suffer, the quality of life with and without hope, are also topics broached by Jean Anouilh in his play *Antigone* (1942), a modern French version or reinterpretation of the ancient Greek tragedy *Antigone* by Sophocles. Antigone, a daughter of Oedipus, defies an edict issued by her uncle Creon, the new king of Thebes. Creon does everything to try and persuade Antigone to fall into line, but when he is unsuccessful he has no option but to put affairs of the state over family loyalty and have her executed. The following exchange comes from their final confrontation:

> ANTIGONE: We are of the tribe that asks questions, and we ask them to the bitter end. Until no tiniest chance of hope remains to be strangled by our hands. We are of the

---

[45]Compare also Doña Rosita in *Doña Rosita la soltera*. After waiting for many years for her fiancé to return to Granada from Argentina so that they can finally be married, she finds out that he is already married to someone else over in America and will not be coming back. In response to this crushing news, she offers this: 'Ya perdí la esperanza de hacerlo [casarme] con quien quise con toda mi sangre, con quien quise y... con quien quiero. Todo está acabado... y, sin embargo, con toda la ilusión perdida, me acuesto, y me levanto con el más terrible de los sentimientos, que es el sentimiento de tener la esperanza muerta. Quiero huir, quiero no ver, quiero quedarme serena, vacía... [...] Y, sin embargo, la esperanza me persigue, me ronda, me muerde; como un lobo moribundo que apretara sus dientes por última vez.'

tribe that hates your filthy hope, your docile, female
hope; hope, your whore —

CREON: […] If you could see how ugly you are,
shrieking those words!

ANTIGONE: Yes, I am ugly! Father was ugly, too. […]
But Father became beautiful. And do you know when?
[…] At the very end. When all his questions had been
answered. When he could no longer doubt that he *had*
killed his own father; that he *had* gone to bed with his
own mother. When all hope was gone, stamped out like a
beetle. When it was absolutely certain that nothing,
nothing could save him. Then he was at peace; then he
could smile, almost; then he became beautiful… (pp.
58–59)[46]

The 'peace' that Antigone says Oedipus experienced is identical to
the certitude, tranquility and ability to sleep that both Yerma and the
Madre say they have attained. Indeed, Anouilh makes a crucial
distinction between melodrama and tragedy:

CHORUS: Tragedy is clean, it is restful, it is flawless. It
has nothing to do with melodrama — with wicked
villains, persecuted maidens, avengers, sudden
revelations and eleventh-hour repentances. Death, in a
melodrama, is really horrible because it is never
inevitable. The dear old father might so easily have been
saved; the honest young man might so easily have
brought in the police five minutes earlier.
    In a tragedy, nothing is in doubt and everyone's
destiny is known. That makes for tranquillity. […]
Tragedy is restful; and the reason is that hope, that foul,
deceitful thing, has no part in it. There isn't any hope.

[46]Jean Anouilh, *Antigone*, translated by Lewis Galantière (London:
Methuen, 1960).

> You're trapped. The whole sky has fallen on you, and all
> you can do about it is to shout. […]
>   In melodrama, you argue and struggle in the hope of
> escape. That is vulgar; it's practical. But in tragedy,
> where there is no temptation to try to escape, argument is
> gratuitous; it's kingly. (pp. 34–35)

When the heroine is tied to the railway tracks and the locomotive is approaching, there is still the possibility, still the hope that at the eleventh hour she will be rescued — this is melodrama (*6*, p. 139); in tragedy, all uncertainty is eliminated and things absolutely have to be a certain way. Furthermore, it is very important to distinguish between the resignation or acceptance ('resignarse', 'conformidad') that Juan and some of the other characters try to urge upon Yerma in the course of the play, and the calm that she finally achieves: acceptance of one's lot implies renouncing hope of change when there is still room for hope, whereas the calmness comes from an absolute state, albeit an entirely negative one, that is to say from knowing that there is nothing left, no avenues unexplored, no possibility still existent, no way out.

    In the subtitle of the play, Lorca defined *Yerma* as a 'Poema trágico en tres actos y seis cuadros' (29); in interviews he referred to it simply as a tragedy: '*Yerma* es una tragedia. […] Yo he querido hacer eso: una tragedia: una tragedia, pura y simplemente' (181; cf. 137, 150, 153, 184). Lorca's motives for turning to this genre are several, and they have to do both with the themes that he wanted to explore and with their mode of expression. First of all, the nature of the subject matter is appropriate to tragedy, and vice versa: '*Yerma* será la tragedia de la mujer estéril' (150–51); '*Yerma* és una tragèdia. Una tragèdia de debò. Des de les primeres escenes, el públic s'adona que passarà quelcom de grandiós' (183); '*Yerma* […] és una tragèdia de cap a cap […] Comencen a parlar els personatges, i ja tot seguit s'endevina que passarà alguna cosa de seriós, de gran' (191). In addition, as we have seen (chapter 7), the notion of fate or destiny that was central to classical tragedy lends itself particularly well to recasting in an existentialist vein, and Lorca presented Yerma the character precisely as the victim of fate. As he commented: 'El tema, como usted sabe, es clásico.[47] Pero yo quiero que tenga un desarrollo y una intención nuevos' (151); '*Yerma*, cuerpo de tragedia que yo he vestido con ropajes modernos, es, sobre todas las cosas, la imagen de la fecundidad castigada a la esterilidad. Un alma en la que se cebó el Destino señalándola para víctima de lo infecundo' (160).

Anouilh's *Antigone* is based directly on Sophocles's play of the same name, and not surprisingly, several critics have sought antecedents for *Yerma* among the corpus of Greek tragedies. For instance, Yerma's name is acoustically similar to those of several Greek protagonists: Phaedra (Fedra in Spanish), Medea, Electra (*29*, p. 292; *3*, p. 20). But Rodríguez Adrados rightly acknowledges that there is no single Greek play that served as a model for *Yerma*. Rather he finds Aeschylus in general to be the Greek tragedian closest to Lorca, in terms of dramatic structure, symbols and themes (*43*, pp. 55–60), and he also detects some similarities between *Yerma* and Euripides's *Hippolytus* (*43*, pp. 60–61; *44*, p. 225). Feal sees a number of persuasive parallels with Euripides's *Bacchae*, where Juan would find his correlative character in Pentheus, who is utterly hostile to Dionysus, and Yerma in Agave, one of the Bacchantes and Pentheus's mother, who kills him at the end of the play during their rites up in the mountains outside Thebes (*21*, pp. 75–80; *39*, p. 16; *44*, pp. 223–24). Sophocles's *Electra* (in Hugo von Hofmannsthal's version) was staged in Madrid in 1931, and Seneca's *Medea* (in Miguel de Unamuno's translation) in Mérida's Roman theatre in 1933; Rosslyn notes that both productions were revived in the summer of 1934 (during a 'Semana Romana' in Mérida), and she detects themes from both of them in *Yerma* (*44*, p. 222).

Clearly, then, there are a number of points of contact and parallels, some likely coincidental, others possible influences. But intriguing as this kind of approach can be, it completely ignores or sidesteps the more fundamental issue of whether tragedy is possible at all in the twentieth century, and specifically in literary

---

[47]Besides classical mythology, Lorca may well be thinking of the biblical stories (chapter 8).

compositions by authors who do not subscribe to an 'ultimately benevolent or at least positive cosmic order' (*46*, p. 202; see chapter 7).[48] Pérez Marchand analyses the most basic difference, namely that the forces at play in Greek tragedy, be they conceived as *moira*, *heimarmene*, or *ananke*, as the Moirai, Zeus, or the four of them acting in conjunction, are supernatural, transcendent and external to human beings, whereas in Lorca, the tragic seed or impulse is located within the individual (*42*, pp. 91–92; see chapter 7).[49]

This radical shift in outlook, from a supernaturally governed and structured world to a godless and arbitrary one, has other implications too, which are most lucidly discussed by Shaw. Because in classical tragedy 'at the end of the play, the audience was expected to achieve some sense of acceptance of necessity or reconciliation with suffering which implied recognition of some over-arching order' (*46*, pp. 202–03), and because that 'order' is lacking in modern tragedy, emphasis shifts away from the denouement and rather 'the playwright's tragic vision has to be expressed by the whole situation, which has no possible satisfactory outcome' (p. 205). Hence, 'in Northrop Frye's terms, it forces the playwright to emphasise tragic *condition*, rather than tragic *process*', and thus, 'within the typology of the genre, Lorca's last great plays are essentially tragedies of *situation*' (p. 205). These observations accord exactly with what has already been noted with regard to the relative lack of plot and the stress on Yerma's predicament. Shaw continues:

---

[48]Lorca was not alone in posing and attempting to answer this question. Valle-Inclán's invention of the new genre of the *esperpento* in 1920 could be seen as his response to what becomes of tragedy in a world without God, gods or noble tragic heroes. In more conventional and less inventive terms, Jacinto Grau had attempted to return to tragedy and breathe new life into the genre with his plays *Entre llamas* (1907/1915), *El conde Alarcos* (1907/1917) and *El hijo pródigo* (1917/1918).

[49]See the entries on 'fate' and 'Fates' in *The Oxford Companion to Classical Literature*, 2nd ed., ed. M. C. Howatson (Oxford: OUP, 1989), p. 232.

...instead of presenting us with a conflict between
equally 'justified' forces, [Lorca's late plays] offer us the
spectacle of a clash between equally 'unjustified' forces.
That is to say: when Lorca undertakes in these plays an
examination of the basic nature of human experience,
with the aim of bringing us to a heightened
understanding of the way things are, his conclusions
leave us in a condition of lost hope. For the protagonists
we feel commiseration rather than admiration. (p. 205)

Thus modern tragedy *is* possible, but it needs to be slightly redefined
in relation to its ancient predecessor and understood on its own
terms:

To the extent that in watching these plays we 'see things
plain' through the spectacle of suffering, what we see are
human beings crushed between passions and repressions
over which they have little control and in circumstances
which produce little positive moral or spiritual change in
the protagonists. This is rather different from the way we
expect to understand older forms of tragedy and is a
mark of Lorca's originality. (pp. 206–07)

Another very different motive that Lorca had for turning to the
genre of tragedy was his great concern with the state of the Spanish
stage in the 1930s, which he felt to be, in large part, stagnant,
intellectually unchallenging and overly commercialized. He was
convinced that, alongside the contributions of innovation and
outright experimentation, another way of reinvigorating
contemporary theatrical life was to return to 'the classics', which for
him meant both Spanish Golden Age drama and ancient Greek
tragedy: 'Hay que volver a la tragedia. Nos obliga a ello la tradición
de nuestro teatro dramático. Tiempo habrá de hacer comedias, farsas.
Mientras tanto, yo quiero dar al teatro tragedias' (151). For his
purposes, therefore, Lorca needed to work out ways of incorporating
key elements of the genre in his own composition, without on the

one hand producing a slavish imitation or on the other straying too far from the established models. Thinking of himself as 'recibiendo la luz de normas antiguas pero eternas en el teatro trágico' (137), he asserted both that 'he procurado guardar fidelidad a los cánones' (181) and '*Yerma* vull creure que és quelcom de nou tot i ésser la tragedia un gènere antic' (184).

In specific and practical terms, then, and beyond the subject matter and themes, this re-creation of tragedy was also based on certain structural features, such as a reduced number of primary characters and, above all, the use of a chorus. Lorca described *Yerma* as 'una tragedia con cuatro personajes principales' (151), and indeed we find that in the history of Greek tragedy 'to the single actor of Thespis' invention Aeschylus added a second and Sophocles a third, and three actors seem to have remained the norm'.[50] In interviews Lorca alluded repeatedly to the use and function of a chorus: 'Una tragedia con [...] coros, como han de ser las tragedias' (151); 'La parte fundamental — claro — reside en los coros, que subrayan la acción de los protagonistas' (181); 'Tal com convé en una tragèdia, he introduit a *Yerma* uns cors que comenten els fets, o el tema de la tragèdia, que és constantment el mateix' (183); '*Yerma* [...] és una tragèdia de cap a cap, amb el cor i totes les coses que aquest gènere comporta' (191); 'El coro lo utilizo para dar el argumento' (197). His most detailed thoughts on the subject are to be found in a newspaper report of 1934; distinguishing between the interior and exterior scenes in the play (see chapter 4), he offered what needs to be recognized as a rather sweeping generalization:

> ...los otros tres [exteriores] [...]. En éstos no intervienen para nada los protagonistas y solamente actúan verdaderos coros a la manera griega. Estos coros, ya iniciados por mí en *Bodas de sangre* — aunque con la timidez de una primera experiencia — , en el cuadro del despertar de la Novia, adquieren en *Yerma* un desarrollo más intenso, una importancia más relevante. (160)

---

[50]*The Oxford Companion to Classical Literature*, p. 577.

While it is hard to conceive of the structure of Act I, Scene ii strictly in terms of a chorus, these observations do apply fully to Act II, Scene i and in large measure to Act III, Scene ii, and it was precisely to the Lavanderas scene that Lorca most frequently referred: 'el primer cuadro del segundo acto, donde yo desarrollo un coro' (137); 'la [escena] de les bugaderes result[e] una cosa excepcional' (183).

Comparing his usage with Greek tragedy, we know that in the latter the chorus was on stage for the duration of the play, while the main actors appeared in the episodes (*epeisodia*, equivalent to scenes) in which they had a part. Furthermore:

> Greek tragedy contained two elements, choral song in lyric metres, with musical accompaniment, and dramatic spoken exchanges between characters, which were mainly in iambic trimeters. Some parts were a blend of the two, spoken or chanted by an actor, solo or with the chorus, to the accompaniment of music (i.e. recitative). These parts were written in tetrameters and iambics interspersed with lyrics. An exchange between an actor and the chorus, each side singing in turn, was known as a *kommos*. The importance of the chorus varied from play to play [...] In general the chorus plays the part of spectators of the action, humble in rank, taking a limited part in but rarely initiating action [...] and commenting on or interpreting the dramatic situation. [...] Very little is known about the dances performed by the chorus after the early fifth century when, we are told, Phrynichus and Aeschylus invented many dances.[51]

In the light of this information, and although, as we have seen, Lorca himself emphasized the scene with the Lavanderas, it is the *romería* scene that actually comes closest to the classical model, with its mixture of poetry and prose and the alternation of dialogue between main characters and the choral sections, with verse, song and dance.

---

[51]*Oxford Companion to Classical Literature*, pp. 76–577; see also *43*, p. 55.

While Lorca clearly drew inspiration for *Yerma* from these ancient sources, nonetheless we should note other principal features of classical tragedy which are missing, muted or altered in Lorca's twentieth-century tragedy. Obviously the circumstances of performance have changed considerably, moving from the open-air structure to the conventional modern theatre with its auditorium and proscenium arch; Greek tragedies were also performed exclusively by male actors all of whom wore masks. As to subject matter and plot, principal characters in Greek tragedy were almost always drawn from mythology, and hence were either of divine or of aristocratic origins, a far cry from the modest farmers of the Spanish village (*34*, p. 227). Yerma's unbending fixation on motherhood could be seen as her tragic flaw or defect (*hamartia*) (*34*, pp. 228, 230; *32*, p. 23), but it is very different from the flaw of excessive pride or over-confidence (*hubris*) that we most often expect to find in the otherwise noble character of the protagonist (for a different view, see *14*, p. 88). The plot feature known as a reversal of fortune (*peripetia*) is completely absent — indeed, the action is defined precisely by the unchanging nature of the situation. On the other hand, there certainly is a kind of recognition scene (*anagnorisis*), in that Yerma is forced to confront the essence of her condition in the last conversation with the Vieja (chapter 7), even though it is something that she has known or half-known, unconsciously or unconfessedly, since the very beginning (*34*, p. 228).

Finally, Shaw's analysis of the underpinnings of modern tragedy has particular implications for the phenomenon of catharsis. Where the audience does not achieve at the denouement 'some sense of acceptance of necessity or reconciliation with suffering' because there is no 'recognition of some over-arching order' (*46*, pp. 202–03), 'the playwright can only succeed in conveying misery or despair, not tragic emotion: tragic pity turns into painful indignation or resigned passivity' (p. 203). This in turn negates 'catharsis as most critics define it, i.e. as something more than simply a heightened state of awareness. It leaves tragic insight itself in the ascendant and the play, viewed as an aesthetic construct, as the only symbol of possible harmony' (p. 204). Such would appear to be the case with *Yerma*: there is surely some fear experienced by the audience as they watch Yerma strangle Juan (*27*, p. 176), she does elicit a measure of pity or commiseration, and she has reached that state of negative certainty untouched by hope (see above, pp. 129-32). But the spectators are left, I would argue, with a profound sense of existential pessimism rather than with the purgation, reconciliation or relief of true catharsis (*42*, p. 92), and if they are to find any uplift or intimations of harmony, then these are located rather in the artistic values and achievement of the play itself (as both literary text and theatre production) (*46*, p. 204).

Taken together, then, these observations demonstrate that Lorca was not interested in creating an exact imitation or some twentieth-century pastiche, but rather in drawing on and connecting with the essence of tragedy (a simple plot, few characters, fate, a predetermined denouement), reinventing the genre in twentieth-century terms (with the implications of the absence of an 'over-arching order' [*46*, p. 203]), as well as exploiting some of the technical features, such as the chorus, that he believed would work effectively on the modern stage.

10. Conclusion

Yerma is a play that, over the years, has been interpreted in a large number of different ways: there have been readings that have stressed any one of many angles, ranging from the mythic or archetypal (*31, 49*) to the psychological, psychoanalytical, medical, anthropological, sociological, socio-political, historical and biographical. Yerma as a character has been held up for our total and unreserved admiration, and she has been fiercely criticized. Juan has been repeatedly attacked and accused of a multitude of defects and shortcomings, but he too has had his occasional defenders.[52] The play has been repeatedly hailed as a masterpiece, and it has also — though less frequently — been found to be an imperfect work of art, with flaws of different kinds that range in seriousness from the minor to the profound. Thus, for instance, Fernández-Cifuentes notes that several of the first-night reviews are perturbed by a 'falta de acción, de desarrollo, de asunto, de cohesión; falta, incluso, de espectáculo' (*22*, p. 166), Pérez Marchand is led to conclude that the play 'carece de interiorización psicológica' (*42*, p. 94), while Valente returns essentially to the initial complaint — 'la [...] falta de calidad dramática' (*53*, p. 198), though his reasoning is now much more elaborate and sophisticated.

One way in which *Yerma* has been read on occasions brings the biographical dimension into play and proposes a kind of psychologizing of the author; despite a number of valid theoretical arguments against any approach of this kind, nevertheless the principal ideas involved here merit brief mention. More than one critic has noticed that there are several references to unborn children in Lorca's poetry, in 'Elegía' from *Libro de poemas*, for example,

---

[52]For a good survey of criticism up to 1974, see *6*; Allen points out the dubious foundations on which much of this criticism has been based.

but perhaps above all in *Suites*: the poems 'Arco de lunas', 'Cancioncilla del niño que no nació' and 'Encuentro' are three of the most obvious examples (*3*, pp. 9–11). In the light of this, it is not hard to arrive at the kind of hypothesis first voiced in a footnote in an early book by J.B. Trend about Lorca:

> One of the critics who was present at the first
> performance of *Yerma* has written to me as follows:
>
> 'La Argentinita, la noche del estreno de *Yerma*, nos
> decía esto: "La obra es la propia tragedia de Federico. A
> él lo que más le gustaría en este mundo es quedar
> embarazado y parir… Es ello lo que verdaderamente
> echa de menos: estar preñado, dar a luz un niño o una
> niña… Yo creo que lo que más le gustaría sería un
> niño… Yerma es Federico, la tragedia de Federico".'[53]

Umbral makes a parallel though not identical point, inasmuch as his rather idiosyncratic interpretation of *Yerma* sees the play not as the tragedy of sterility but rather of 'la libido frustrada':

> Si hay un erotismo superfluo que excede de las
> necesidades de la criatura y de la especie, he aquí que en
> Yerma encontramos una forma aún más inexplicable de
> superfluidad: el erotismo que ni siquiera cumple esas
> necesidades. […] Yerma es la libido frustrada, como es
> frustrada la libido de los invertidos de ambos sexos o la
> libido insaciable. (Y por aquí empezaríamos a identificar
> a la criatura con su creador, aquí podría llevarnos el
> personaje a la busca de su autor.) (*52*, pp. 175–76)

But it is José Ángel Valente who has argued most eloquently for this way of understanding the play. Valente suggests that for Lorca homosexuality implied the impossibility of fathering a child, an

---

[53]J. B. Trend, *Lorca and the Spanish Poetic Tradition* (Oxford: Basil Blackwell, 1956), p. 23, n. 19.

impossibility which he found particularly painful because procreation is for the adult a means — albeit partial — of both recovering one's lost childhood and compensating for one's future death (*53*, p. 195; see *51*, p. 108 and chapter 7). Consequently, and unlike the heterosexual, the homosexual experiences a 'complicidad [...] de la muerte y de la no seminalidad del eros' (p. 198). Hence, as far as *Yerma* is concerned, Valente sees the result in Freudian terms:

> ...no entendemos que haya propiamente en *Yerma* un proceso sublimatorio, sino un neto desplazamiento argumental del llanto por lo estéril (manifiestamente condicionado por la relación homosexual) que ya había encontrado expresión abierta, más eficaz y más propia en la escritura precedente de Lorca. (p. 199)

A very different approach but still one with, as it were, an author-based focus suggests that the play needs to be read figuratively as a transposition and expression of writerly concerns. According to this view, Yerma stands for the author, the dramatist, and her desire to procreate mirrors the desire to compose, to create a literary work. The play thus comes to be about the nature of the creative act and the necessary preconditions for successful creation/composition (*6*, pp. 143, 146, 153). Yerma's inhibitions and her excessive self-reflexivity prevent her from procreating, and likewise the writer who is overly cerebral and controlling and who does not give free play to his imagination will not be able to create (*6*, pp. 145–47, 154; *40*, p. 66). In figurative, and perhaps also literal, terms Yerma needs to sing, to be able to sing, in order to conceive, and so too the poet or writer (*40*, p. 65). Ter Horst, however, sees a quite distinct analogy: for him it is Juan who is the artist, his land and livestock the canvas with which he paints, successfully prospering and multiplying, while, in order 'to be able to create in breadth and depth, [he] only grudgingly expends sexually a vital substance' (*50*, p. 50).

Shifting attention now away from the author and on to the protagonist, but at the same time returning to a model that involves speculative psychological analysis, other critics see Yerma's problem not essentially as frustrated motherhood, but rather as repressed sexuality or libido, her barrenness resulting in some way from this or being the visible manifestation of that more deep-lying condition (*2*, p. 32; *6*; *8*, pp. 45, 53; *52*). But repressed sexuality would be at the heart of the play only if the connection between taking unalloyed pleasure in eroticism and achieving pregnancy were actually, scientifically, medically true, rather than just a widely-held folk belief. Honour, too, has sometimes been taken as a primary theme of *Yerma*, rather than seen as what it really is, a major complicating factor, that happens to loom large in Yerma's value-system, but not a theme in its own right. Yerma's repressed libido is like honour in that it makes Yerma's life that much more difficult, but it is not at the heart of the play: she is less able to tolerate a childless life with Juan because their sexual relations afford her no personal satisfaction and no physical pleasure, and sexual repression is one factor, among several (including honour), in eliminating from the realm of possibility other potential solutions (adultery, separation, abandonment) to her predicament.

From a very different methodological perspective, yet other lines of interpretation that have been put forward with some regularity involve a heavy emphasis on historical, political and sociological considerations. One such reading portrays Lorca as, first and foremost, a committed liberal social reformer: according to this kind of approach, Yerma lives in a backward and repressive society, and Lorca is taking aim at the social, political and religious forces that impede change. If Yerma were better educated, if wives were not so subject to their husbands, if divorce existed and were accepted, the argument goes, then her problem would be solved. But this standpoint pays no attention to what, for want of a better word, we may term the philosophical side of the play (*27*, p. 155). The cycles of nature and human mortality are just two of a number of immutable factors that are left untouched by political reform and social change, and given that the play is indeed a tragedy that connects with the classical tradition, that certain things cannot be altered — like Yerma's own name —, it seems clear where the stress ultimately lies. I believe that in the 1930s Lorca found himself increasingly in a dilemma, for on the one hand he did subscribe to many of the ideals and reformist policies of the Second Republic, but on the other he was philosophically a pessimist (*27*, pp. 157, 174; *35*, p. 237).[54] He would certainly have supported improving the living conditions and the quality of life of *campesinos* throughout Spain, but those improvements would not have the slightest impact on certain eternal verities concerning the human condition (*4*, p. 18; *27*, p. 158).

If we turn from the socio-political to another, closely related way of reading the play, namely the anthropological, the underlying problem that emerges here is that Yerma and Juan are not what could be described as typical or representative characters, just as Bernarda from *La casa de Bernarda Alba* is not (*17*, *passim*). That is to say, the personality, behaviour and value-system of Yerma and Juan are sufficiently normative to allow us to recognize them as functional members of this Spanish village where the action is set, yet they are at the same time sufficiently non-normative to rule out seeing them as figures who are truly representative of the community to which they belong. This is immediately clear with regard to Yerma: her desire for children within marriage is absolutely typical, but the intensity of that desire, to say nothing of her single-mindedness, unrelenting stubbornness and complete unwillingness to compromise at any cost, are absolutely untypical. At first sight Juan's oddness within this society draws less attention to itself, for he subscribes to many of its unwritten laws, but his inability to rule his wife, and above all his disregard for heirs, mark him out, like Yerma, as someone who does not fully meet a norm of expected attitudes and priorities (*1*, p. 32).[55] After all, if Juan were as concerned as his wife

---

[54]See my article, 'El último Lorca: unas aclaraciones a *La casa de Bernarda Alba, Sonetos* y *Drama sin título*', in *Lecciones sobre Federico García Lorca*, ed. Andrés Soria Olmedo (Granada: Comisión del Cincuentenario, 1986), pp. 131–45.

[55]As Corbin says of *La casa de Bernarda Alba*, 'Bernarda and her family are products of their culture, but other, happier, products are possible' (*17*, p. 714).

is about having children, as would be typical in this society, then there would simply be no play, either because the two of them would try harder and eventually procreate successfully, or because they would be united in the suffering and mutual sympathy occasioned by their shared childlessness (*11*, p. 78; *23*, p. 354).

It may well be that this degree of behavioural or psychological oddness that we can observe in both of them makes Yerma and Juan particularly suitable as the protagonists of a tragedy (*8*, p. 53). On the one hand they are larger than life, which focusses attention on a particular set of problems and enhances the artistic impact on the audience, while on the other they are still credible members of their community. They are not so divorced from reality that we are unable to identify with them, at least up to a point.

This subtle blend of the normative and the non-normative evidenced in the characters of Yerma and Juan is mirrored exactly in the play as a whole, inasmuch as *Yerma*, like a high proportion of Lorca's other dramatic works, is based on a mixture of realism and symbolism. Many facets of Yerma's world have been drawn from a reality that Lorca himself knew and had experienced at first hand: the land, farming, irrigation, daily life in a small Spanish village, social pressures and constraints — these are all painted accurately and vividly. The scene with the washerwomen is based on memories of a visit that Lorca made in 1926 to Cáñar, a small village in the Alpujarras mountains, where, as he tells his correspondent, he saw 'lavanderas cantando'.[56] The details of the *romería* are drawn from a yearly pilgrimage at Moclín, a small town about fifteen miles northwest of Granada, situated at the edge of the Vega in the foothills of the Sierra Elvira (*23*, pp. 356–57; *29*, p. 306; *36*, pp. 31–33; *38*, pp. 69–70). In real life the shrine is dedicated to the Cristo del Paño, a feature that Lorca has softened in his literary treatment by substituting a nameless saint. Furthermore, some of the songs and other features can be traced to a variety of regions within Spain (*23*, p. 357; *29*, pp. 305–06).

---

[56]*Epistolario completo*, ed. Andrew A. Anderson & Christopher Maurer (Madrid: Cátedra, 1997), p. 330.

At the same time, it is equally obvious that the play is far from offering a rigorous anthropological document. I have already commented on Yerma and Juan. Víctor plays out his allotted supporting role; neither he nor Juan presents a fully-rounded three-dimensional psychological portrait, and rather each is fleshed out just sufficiently for the purposes of their function within the plot. Each one of the minor characters represents a distinctive attitude and/or set of circumstances with respect to marriage and children, so that taken as a group they offer a whole array of possibilities. For the rest, the village and its inhabitants disappear into a barely glimpsed and distant background, and a large majority of the other aspects of village life are never even touched upon. In the strategic sequence of the six scenes, we can clearly detect the hand of the author, offering a carefully calculated progression of brief episodes extracted from Yerma's life (*34*, p. 227). And as we saw in chapter 5, there is a seamless transition in the way in which elements from the natural world surrounding the characters acquire a strong and sometimes plurivalent symbolic force in their dialogue.

The statements that Lorca made in interviews reflect this intermediate status of the play, located somewhere between the poles of realism and symbolism. Thus, on one occasion he asserted that:

> De la realidad son fruto las dos obras [*Bodas de sangre* y *Yerma*]. Reales son sus figuras; rigurosamente auténtico el tema de cada una de ellas... Primero, notas, observaciones tomadas de la vida misma, del periódico a veces... (175)

But while this is true, it is really only half the story. Thus on another occasion he could equally well affirm that 'Els actors no parlen amb naturalitat. Res de naturalitat' (183). Lorca resolved this apparent contradiction in the following comment:

> Son reales, desde luego. Pero todo tipo real encarna un símbolo. Y yo pretendo hacer de mis personajes un

hecho poético, aunque los haya visto alentar alrededor
mío. Son una realidad estética. (194)

That is to say, they are both/and, they perform a double duty. The
characters are drawn from reality and rooted in reality, but
simultaneously they symbolize more — sometimes much more —
than their literal self. Consequently, Lorca envisaged the appeal of
his work on two distinct levels:

> Mi teatro tiene dos planos: una vertiente del poeta, que
> analiza y que hace que sus personajes se encuentren para
> producir la idea subterránea, que yo doy al 'buen
> entendedor', y el plano natural de la línea melódica, que
> toma el público sencillo para quien mi teatro físico es un
> gozo, un ejemplo y siempre una enseñanza. El hombre
> que dice que 'ahonde' el marido, a la mujer marchita,
> expresa una doble idea, como la que surge de la
> interpretación del crepúsculo. Mientras para el
> campesino es un signo exterior del Universo, en el que
> agoniza la luz y le señala la hora de cesar en el trabajo y
> de comer, el espectador agudo y sentidor se ve
> reposando en un ataúd con los gusanos eternos. (198)

There were several advantages to this kind of strategy of
composition, including a broad appeal to a wide public, as well as
being able to avoid the dangers of falling, on the one hand, into sheer
entertainment or anecdotalism, and on the other into pure
abstraction. If we recall how Lorca conceptualized these two levels
in his work, as 'tipo real / símbolo' and 'realidad / estética', we can
see how the pair 'real / real simbólico' falls into this same paradigm
and appreciate exactly what he means by 'ideas vestidas':

> La raíz de mi teatro es calderoniana. Teatro de magia. En
> la romería de *Yerma* salto de lo real a lo real simbólico,
> en el sentido poético de obtener ideas vestidas, no puros
> símbolos. (196)

This blend of realism and symbolism is also reflected in other ways, such as the mixture of prose and verse used in the text (chapter 4). For the most part, then, the dialogue is naturalistic, with conversations about agricultural tasks, meals, household chores and village gossip, but the repeated shift to verse and with it a denser figurative language heightens our awareness that the action and the characters also point to much broader issues far beyond their individual lives. The controlled artistic quality of all that is presented on stage is also underlined by Lorca's concerns regarding the pace and timing of the action and the performance. As he himself said:

> El coro lo utilizo para dar el argumento. Trato de evitar que el poeta desmenuce su sentido preciso, para no incurrir en lentitud, porque tengo la preocupación de que todo tenga un gran ritmo. (197)

Perhaps the risk of creating the impression of excessive slowness was greater because Lorca was, at the same time, aiming at producing a feeling of monotony:

> Aunque para mí lo más interesante de mi drama es el proceso obsesivo de la mujer, que habla igual desde que sale hasta que desaparece, y que he cuidado de acompañarla de una musicalidad monótona. (196)

Clearly, then, timing, the timing of actions and speeches, of entrances and exits, was crucial in bringing about the desired effect:

> Calculo que dentro de este mes quedará lista para el estreno mi tragedia *Yerma*. Los ensayos andan bastante adelantados. Hace falta mucho y muy cuidadoso ensayo para conseguir el ritmo que debe presidir la representación de una obra dramática. [...] Margarita Xirgu, que tiene en *Yerma* un papel en el que puede demostrar todas las enormes cualidades de su excepcional temperamento, pone el mayor interés en que

este ritmo sea logrado. Lo mismo hacen los actores y
actrices que la acompañan. (153–154)

Likewise, the visual impact of the scenes, with the combination of
the stage sets, the costumes, and the disposition and movement of
actors, particularly when in groups, was another significant
consideration. Referring to the *romería* scene, one of Lorca's
interviewers asserted that 'Es un quadre d'una plasticitat
obsessionant' (182), and Lorca concurred: 'Aquesta escena i la de les
bugaderes resulten una cosa excepcional' (183).

The bulk of these observations hold true for the two other
plays in the trilogy, *Bodas de sangre* and *La casa de Bernarda Alba*,
as well as for *Doña Rosita la soltera* (composed immediately after
Yerma), and, to a greater or lesser extent, for several other plays by
Lorca. For instance, *La zapatera prodigiosa* and *Amor de don
Perlimplín con Belisa en su jardín* also employ prose dialogue
punctuated by verse and song, but in these two cases the overall
degree of stylization is higher, and the characters and the action are
rather more distant from the humdrum reality of everyday life. On
the other hand, *La zapatera prodigiosa* enjoys a particular
connection with *Yerma* in that the situation of the two protagonists is
in some measure the same: both women find themselves in
mismatched marriages, and both will remain childless. But because
La zapatera prodigiosa is a farce and not a tragedy, and because the
Zapatera has a very different character, the denouement turns out
very differently.

The other Lorca play that also contains at its centre the motif
of the unborn child is *Así que pasen cinco años* (1931), one of his
more experimental works and stylistically quite distinct from *Yerma*
(*53*, p. 194). However, despite all the differences, Valente sees
Yerma as an 'extrapolación argumental' of *Así que pasen* (p. 198). In
this earlier play the male protagonist, the Joven, fails to make a
connection with the women in his life at the right moment, and so
opportunities are missed and he ends up never marrying and never
having children. The notion of potential (but unfulfilled)
childbearing is most to the fore in the fantastic scene played out

between the Joven and a shop-window display mannequin dressed in a sumptuous wedding gown. In lyrical language set in verse the Maniquí insinuates what could have been, from the consummation of the wedding night through to the birth of a child, the Joven realizes that this is what he wants too, and he rushes off at the end of the scene, but of course within the context of the play it is already too late, the dice have already been cast.

All of Lorca's plays, including *Yerma*, communicate in what might be called an allegorical fashion, allegorical in the sense that the particular situation and story of the characters and their actions correspond to and lead us to apprehend some broader and more general truth. This element is perhaps clearest in his earliest dramatic work, *El maleficio de la mariposa*, where all the characters are insects and the plot revolves around the impossible love of the protagonist — a cockroach — for a beautiful butterfly. The kind of interpretative leap that needs to be made, from the concrete, literal level of the play's content to the abstract, figurative level of the play's theme, is different in every case and, as has already been suggested, in *Yerma* there is perhaps less distance between the two levels than in any other play. But this makes for much of the immediacy of its impact. While Yerma's predicament is far from everyone's, her claim to basic human rights, her struggle for self-realization, her resistance to compromise, her need to maintain her integrity intact, and her desire to survive or perpetuate herself, all of these surely are issues of universal concern.

Bibliographical Note

Besides the latest version of Mario Hernández's Alianza edition of *Yerma* (listed as 5 below), which is the text that I have used in the preparation of this Guide, there are several other worthwhile editions of the play, which appear in the first section of the Bibliography below.

The amount of existing criticism on *Yerma* is very considerable indeed. Just about every general study of Lorca has a section or chapter devoted to the play, as does every book specifically concerned with his drama. Most editions also offer a critical introduction, of varying length. In addition, there are nearly one hundred articles, published in academic journals and magazines, that are concerned with the play (or with one or other of its theatrical productions), to say nothing of the dozens of further articles that treat *Yerma* within the context of the 'rural trilogy' or Lorca's overall dramatic output. As a result, the list of critical items appearing here is necessarily highly selective.

EDITIONS

1. *Yerma*, ed. Ildefonso-Manuel Gil, Letras Hispánicas, 46, 3rd ed. (Madrid: Cátedra, 1978). A widely used edition; both the text and introduction are a little outdated, but the latter is still useful.
2. *Yerma*, translated with an introduction and notes by Ian Macpherson and Jacqueline Minett, and with a general introduction by John Lyon (Warminster: Aris & Phillips, 1987). A bilingual edition; both introductions are sound and insightful.
3. *Yerma*, ed. Miguel García-Posada, Col. Austral, 80 (Madrid: Espasa-Calpe, 1989). The introduction contains several points of interest.
4. *Yerma*, ed. Robin Warner (Manchester: Manchester University Press, 1994). A very up-to-date edition; the strong introduction is slanted a little towards a socio-political perspective.
5. *Yerma*, ed. Mario Hernández, revised and expanded ed. (Madrid: Alianza, 1998). This edition offers the most reliable text of the play; the introduction is not critical, but rather concerned with the composition and transmission of the text and the premiere of the play.

CRITICISM

6. Allen, Rupert C., *Psyche and Symbol in the Theater of Federico García Lorca: 'Perlimplín', 'Yerma', 'Blood Wedding'* (Austin: University of Texas Press, 1974). An idiosyncratic study; some sections of it are very useful and suggestive, others marginally so.

7. Álvarez Harvey, María Luisa, 'Lorca's Yerma: Frigid ... or Mismatched?', *College Language Association Journal*, 23.4 (1980), 460–69. An approach predicated on much speculation, some of it very far-fetched, but occasionally thought-provoking.

8. Anderson, Reed, 'The Idea of Tragedy in García Lorca's *Yerma*', *Hispanófila*, no.74 (enero 1982), 41–60. An important, substantial, and tightly argued study whose conclusions are rather different from my own.

9   Babín, María Teresa, 'Narciso y la esterilidad en la obra de García Lorca', *Revista Hispánica Moderna*, 11.1–2 (1945), 48–51. A short piece that focusses on Yerma's Narcissism.

10. Benítez, Frank, 'Tensión poética en *Yerma* de García Lorca', *Explicación de Textos Literarios*, 4.1 (1975), 39–45. Proposes an intriguing way of structurally analysing the play.

11. Bobes Naves, María del Carmen, 'Lectura semiológica de *Yerma*', in *Lecturas del texto dramático: variaciones sobre la obra de Lorca* (Oviedo: Universidad de Oviedo & Ateneo Obrero de Gijón, 1990), pp. 67–86. The theoretical underpinnings of the semiological analysis are over-elaborated, but it does make a few perceptive points.

12. Borel, Jean-Paul, *Théâtre de l'impossible: essai sur une des dimensions fondamentales du théâtre espagnol au XXe siècle* (Neuchâtel: Éditions de la Baconnière, 1963). A fine study, particularly good on the themes and broader implications of the play.

13. Cannon, Calvin, 'The Imagery of Lorca's *Yerma*', *Modern Language Quarterly*, 21.2 (1960), 122–30. A lucid and detailed analysis; together with *14*, *32* and *47*, also published in the 1960s, it establishes much of the groundwork and identifies many of the issues for subsequent criticism.

14. ——, '*Yerma* as Tragedy', *Symposium*, 16.2 (1962), 85–93. A thoughtful and well-argued study, strong on the origins and implications of Yerma's tragic predicament.

15. Carbonell Basset, Delfín, 'Tres dramas existenciales de F. García Lorca', *Cuadernos Hispanoamericanos*, 190 (1965), 118–30. While focussing perhaps too narrowly on Heidegger, nonetheless the essay points out some all-too-rarely noted coincidences and parallels.

16. Carrillo Urdanivia, Graciela, 'El teatro de Federico García Lorca: Yerma y su obsesión de inmortalidad', *3 [Tres]* (Lima, Perú), 1.6

(1940), 79–81. A very brief but strikingly insightful account, stressing Unamuno and *Del sentimiento trágico de la vida*.

17. Corbin, John, 'Lorca's *Casa*', *Modern Language Review*, 95.3 (2000), 712–27. An excellent piece based in anthropology, it provides much fascinating background information for all three plays of the rural trilogy and proposes a compelling vision of the character Bernarda.

18. Correa, Gustavo, '*Yerma*: estudios estilísticos sobre la obra de Federico García Lorca', *Revista de las Indias*, 35.109 (1949), 11–63. Contains a long section on different notions of honour; also studies some of the imagery.

19. Cueto, Ronald, *Souls in Anguish: Religion and Spirituality in Lorca's Theatre* (Leeds: Leeds Iberian Papers, Trinity and All Saints College, 1994). A somewhat quirky treatment that nevertheless rightly focusses attention on the Christian background and symbolism.

20. Falconieri, John V., 'Tragic Hero in Search of a Role: *Yerma*'s Juan', *Revista de Estudios Hispánicos* (USA), 1.1 (1967), 17–33. An attempt to rehabilitate Juan and present him as the wronged party; while ultimately unconvincing, it does oblige us to question and refresh our perspective and assumptions.

21. Feal, Carlos, *Lorca: tragedia y mito* (Ottawa: Dovehouse Editions, 1989). Sees the play in archetypal terms; after exploring Freudian and biblical angles, the strongest section draws parallels with Euripides's *Bacchae*.

22. Fernández Cifuentes, Luis, *García Lorca en el teatro: la norma y la diferencia* (Zaragoza: Universidad de Zaragoza, 1986). An acute and sophisticated study that uses the critical reception of the play's premiere as its point of departure.

23. García Lorca, Francisco, *Federico y su mundo*, ed. Mario Hernández, 2nd ed. (Madrid: Alianza, 1981). Worthwhile for a number of reasons, not least the family connection; good background information and sound, conventional interpretation.

24. Gil, Ildefonso-Manuel, 'Yerma: desarrollo de un carácter', in *El teatro y su crítica*, ed. Manuel Alvar (Málaga: Instituto de Cultura de la Diputación Provincial, 1975), pp. 245–58. A solid, thoughtful study that complements the introduction to his edition (*1*).

25. Gilmour, John, 'The Cross of Pain and Death: Religion in the Rural Tragedies', in *Lorca: Poet and Playwright: Essays in Honour of J. M. Aguirre*, ed. Robert Havard (Cardiff: University of Wales Press, 1992), pp. 133–55. A balanced and insightful analysis of religious content and symbolism in the three plays.

26. González-del-Valle, Luis, *La tragedia en el teatro de Unamuno, Valle-Inclán y García Lorca* (New York: Eliseo Torres, 1975). A middle-of-the-road contribution offering some interesting observations.

27. Greenfield, Sumner M., *Lorca, Valle-Inclán y las estéticas de la disidencia: ensayos sobre literatura hispánica* (Boulder, CO: Society of Spanish and Spanish-American Studies, 1996). This volume collects a number of previously published articles; three are relevant to *Yerma*, and together they contain much excellent exegesis which is particularly illuminating with regard to themes and the notion of tragedy.

28. Hernández, Mario, 'La muchacha dorada por la luna', *Trece de Nieve*, 2ª época, nos 1–2 (diciembre 1976), 211–20. A study of Lorca's poem 'Casida de la muchacha dorada' which has a number of points in common with the *romería* scene.

29. ——, 'Cronología y estreno de *Yerma, poema trágico*, de García Lorca', *Revista de Archivos, Bibliotecas y Museos*, 82.2 (1979), 299–315. The best documented account of the composition of the play and its initial critical reception, it complements the material in Hernández's edition (*5*).

30. Klein, Dennis A., 'Christological Imagery in Lorca's *Yerma*', *García Lorca Review*, 6.1 (1978), 35–42. A straightforward treatment of the topic.

31. Knapp, Bettina L., 'Federico García Lorca's *Yerma*: A Woman's Mystery', in *Women in Twentieth-Century Literature: A Jungian View* (University Park, PA: Pennsylvania State University Press, 1987), pp. 11–23. An approach that stresses the archetypal elements, with a number of useful observations on the biblical resonances.

32. Lott, Robert E., '*Yerma*: The Tragedy of Unjust Barrenness', *Modern Drama*, 8.1 (1965), 20–27. An important and substantial article in the middle ground of interpretative possibilities.

33. Martín, Eutimio, *Federico García Lorca, heterodoxo y mártir: análisis y proyección de la obra juvenil inédita* (Madrid: Siglo Veintiuno, 1986). The relevant chapter returns to the reception of the play at its premiere (see *22* and *29*) and adds interesting new material; thence it proceeds to consider Yerma in light of Fray Luis's *La perfecta casada*.

34. Martínez Lacalle, Guadalupe, '*Yerma*: "Una tragedia pura y simplemente"', *Neophilologus*, 72.2 (1988), 227–37. One of the best middle-of-the-road articles from the 1980s, with many telling points within its broad focus on tragedy.

35. McDermott, Patricia, '*Yerma*: extra naturam nulla salus', in *A Face Not Turned to the Wall: Essays on Hispanic Themes for Gareth Alban Davies*, ed. C. A. Longhurst (Leeds: Department of Spanish and Portuguese, University of Leeds, 1987), pp. 235–48. A wide-ranging piece, it is strong on the religious background and content, with a comparison of *Yerma* and Fra Angelico's painting of the Annunciation as well as a demonstration of the many underlying pagan elements in the play.

36. Mora Guarnido, José, *Federico García Lorca y su mundo: testimonio para una biografía* (Buenos Aires: Losada, 1958). Contains an important description of the *romería* at Moclín.

37. Morris, C. B., 'Lorca's *Yerma*: Wife Without an Anchor', *Neophilologus*, 56.3 (1972), 285–97. An important, substantial article, with a host of acute observations.

38. ——, 'Lorca's Yerma and the "beso sabroso"', *Mester* (Los Angeles), 10.1–2 (1981), 68–81. An excellent study of sexuality in the play, focussed on the denouement scene.

39. ——, 'Yerma, abandonada e incompleta', in *El teatro de Lorca: tragedia, drama y farsa*, ed. Cristóbal Cuevas García & Enrique Baena (Málaga: Publicaciones del Congreso de Literatura Española Contemporánea, 1996), pp. 15–41. Another fine piece, building on the two previous contributions.

40. Newton, Candelas, *Understanding Federico García Lorca* (Columbia, SC: University of South Carolina Press, 1995). A very reliable introductory account.

41. Parker, Fiona, & Terence McMullan, 'Federico García Lorca's *Yerma* and the World of Work', *Neophilologus*, 74.1 (1990), 58–69. An exhaustive study of the topic, the article makes a compelling case for this neglected aspect of the play which in turn produces many fresh interpretative insights.

42. Pérez Marchand, Monelisa Lina, 'Apuntes sobre el concepto de la tragedia en la obra dramática de García Lorca', *Asomante*, 4.1 (1948), 86–96. An intelligent and well-documented comparison of the conceptual underpinnings of classical Greek tragedy and those of Lorca's trilogy.

43. Rodríguez Adrados, Francisco, 'Las tragedias de García Lorca y los griegos', *Estudios Clásicos*, 31 (1989), 51–61. In contrast to *42*, the focus here is rather more on structural coincidences; in addition more attention is given to considering a number of specific Greek tragedies as potential analogues.

44. Rosslyn, Felicity, 'Lorca and Greek Tragedy', *Cambridge Quarterly*, 29 (2000), 215–36. The article goes over a lot of ground already covered in different ways in *21*, *42*, *43* and *46*, with occasional further observations of interest.

45. Sánchez Díaz, Carlos, 'Sobre la infecundidad de Yerma', *Anuario de Filología* (Maracaibo), 4 (1965), 247–59. A much more sophisticated study than most of the fault/blame issue.

46. Shaw, Donald L., 'Lorca's Late Plays and the Idea of Tragedy', in *Essays on Hispanic Themes in Honour of Edward C. Riley*, ed. Jennifer Lowe & Philip Swanson (Edinburgh: Department of Hispanic Studies, University of Edinburgh, 1989), pp. 200–08. The best treatment of the topic, relatively brief but extremely perceptive and thought-provoking,

it goes beyond George Steiner's *The Death of Tragedy* and makes many valuable suggestions for conceptualizing twentieth-century tragedy.

47. Skloot, Robert, 'Theme and Image in Lorca's *Yerma*', *Drama Survey*, 5.2 (1966), 151–61. A solid, useful piece, building on *13*, *14* and *32*.

48. Smith, Paul Julian, *The Theatre of García Lorca: Text, Performance, Psychoanalysis* (Cambridge: Cambridge University Press, 1998). Contains fascinating information on early-twentieth-century medical theories of infertility in Spain, and suggests that Yerma may be a transposition of Gregorio Marañón's theories of intersexuality.

49. Sullivan, Patricia, 'The Mythic Tragedy of *Yerma*', *Bulletin of Hispanic Studies*, 49.3 (1972), 265–78. The most abstract mythic/archetypal reading of the play, seeing Juan as Sky-God and Yerma as Mother-Earth who fail to fulfil their destiny.

50. Ter Horst, Robert, 'Nature Against Nature in *Yerma*', in *The World of Nature in the Works of Federico García Lorca*, ed. Joseph W. Zdenek (Rock Hill, SC: Winthrop College, 1980), pp. 43–54. Focusses on nature and the agricultural background and imagery, with helpful comments but also some idiosyncratic readings.

51. Tubert, Silvia, 'La esterilidad como deconstrucción de la maternidad', in *Mujeres sin sombra: maternidad y tecnología* (Madrid: Siglo XXI, 1991), pp. 104–25. A study permeated by modern theory and terminology, it uses Yerma as a model to analyse a range of underlying cultural assumptions and the structures and constraints of traditional society.

52. Umbral, Francisco, *Lorca, poeta maldito* (Barcelona: Editorial Bruguera, 1977). First published in 1968, the book proposes a somewhat off-beat interpretation that is thought-provoking precisely because of its freshness.

53. Valente, José Ángel, 'Pez luna', *Trece de Nieve*, 2ª época, nos 1–2 (diciembre 1976), 191–201. The best example of a certain kind of biographically-based criticism, the study offers many suggestive local comments as well as laying the groundwork for a global rethinking of Lorca's dramatic practice and achievement.

54. Vázquez, Mary S., '*Yerma* de Lorca, historia de una pasión: *natura, naturaleza, naturalidad*', in *Federico García Lorca en el espejo del tiempo*, ed. Pedro Guerrero Ruiz (Alicante: Caja de Ahorros del Mediterráneo & Editorial Aguaclara, 1998), pp. 127–42. The title is slightly misleading, as the article is primarily concerned with drawing out the ambivalences and dichotomies of imagery that inform both action and theme.

CRITICAL GUIDES TO SPANISH TEXTS

Edited by
Alan Deyermond and Stephen Hart

CRITICAL GUIDES TO SPANISH TEXTS

Edited by
Alan Deyermond and Stephen Hart